Healed

HOW MARY MAGDALENE
WAS MADE WELL

Kate Moorehead

Church Publishing
NEW YORK

Church Publishing
19 East 34th Street
New York, NY 10016
www.churchpublishing.org

Cover art: Robert Garrigus / Alamy Stock Photo
Cover design by Jennifer Kopec, 2Pug Design
Typeset by Rose Design

Library of Congress Cataloging-in-Publication Data

Names: Moorehead, Kate, 1970– author.
Title: Healed : how Mary Magdelene was made well / Kate Moorehead.
Description: New York : Church Publishing, 2018.
Identifiers: LCCN 2017036398 (print) | LCCN 2017048685 (ebook) | ISBN 9780898690712 (ebook) | ISBN 9780898690705 (pbk.)
Subjects: LCSH: Mary Magdalene, Saint. | Healing—Religious aspects—Christianity.
Classification: LCC BS2485 (ebook) | LCC BS2485 .M66 2018 (print) | DDC 226/.092—dc23
LC record available at https://lccn.loc.gov/2017036398

Printed in the United States of America

Contents

Introduction

When I graduated from seminary, my husband and I traveled to Israel and Egypt. We did it on the cheap, staying in places and doing things that make us laugh (and cringe) when we look back on it some twenty-two years later. One of the highlights of our trip was backpacking through the Sinai Peninsula. In that wondrous place, which looks more like the moon than a place on earth, the air is so dry that your sweat evaporates the second it reaches the surface of your skin. I was terrified that I would die of dehydration. We wore high-tech lightweight pants and shirts, hiking boots, hats, and backpacks. Our guide was a Bedouin named Jabali´ (literally "mountain man") who wore nothing but flip flops and an off-white, flowing robe, which stayed remarkably clean during our trek through the dusty Sinai wilderness. His simple garment shone in stark contrast to our dirty, ripped clothing (for which we had spent a good part of our trip budget). While we sweated and grunted and heaved our bodies over rocks and boulders the size of trucks, the Bedouin seemed to float over it all. He would walk ahead of us quietly, then turn around, smile, and say "*Shwaya, shwaya*"—which roughly translates "slowly, slowly" or "little by little." He led us to hidden wadis (or oases) that I never thought could have existed in that barren wasteland. There, we found water, and he would brew tea for us over a fire made from dried camel dung. He kept us alive.

A saint is someone who walks ahead of us, guiding us and keeping us on the path to life. The journey to know God can be a perilous one with lots of wrong turns. Sometimes we equip ourselves with all the wrong materials, and sometimes we try to rush things that cannot be rushed. The saints walk ahead of us, showing us new ways to become intimate with God. For us, they are role models. Like us, they struggle and journey, but they drew closer, and each one of them carved out a different path to God.

There is one saint who has been strangely misunderstood for centuries, preventing many of us from having the guide we need to show us the way to God. This saint is Mary Magdalene.

For centuries, Mary Magdalene has been depicted as a prostitute, a wayward woman who was cured by Jesus of her sexual immorality and then became a follower. But Mary was not a prostitute. Not once does the Bible use that word to describe her or even hint of her being a sexually promiscuous woman. Mary Magdalene had demons. She struggled with mysterious illnesses of body and mind. Mary Magdalene suffered the weight of mental health problems. And Jesus healed her.

It is my hope and prayer that telling the truth of her story might allow Mary Magdalene to take her rightful place as the guide for those of us who struggle with mental health issues (and if we are truly honest, that means each and every one of us). Even today, there is so much shame associated with mental illness. Many are still afraid to admit that they suffer in this way. How much would it help us if we embraced the fact that the first person to witness the resurrection lived much of her life fighting a battle against the demons of mental illness?

Jesus chose Mary Magdalene—above all others—to tell the world that he had risen. He chose her as his first witness. He loved and valued her that much, just as he loves and values all who struggle with destructive thoughts and emotions. Mary Magdalene was not a temptress. She was a courageous woman who walked from darkness, fear, and torment into the light of Jesus's healing presence. She stayed with Jesus through his own pain and suffering, even when his disciples ran away. In many ways, she became his closest confidant.

I write this book as a labor of love—for Mary Magdalene and for everyone who suffers from the darkness and fear of mental illness. It is time for us to reclaim a saint of the church and let her show us her beautiful, unique, and sometimes frightening path to true health. It is a path that leads directly to the heart of God.

1

~

Making a Woman

I was the first woman to lead all three of the churches that I have served. I don't know if my leadership is supposed to look different than a man's. My husband used to pump me up when I first came to St. John's Cathedral. "Be the Dean!" he would say. I would try not to slouch. I would try to sound confident and tough. But really, I didn't know what I was supposed to be doing. I have been like a blind person groping my way towards some uniquely feminine form of leadership. To tell you the truth, I often didn't think much about it until I started doing retreats for women and they began asking me about what it was like to be a woman leader in the church.

I found myself searching the Bible for answers to their questions about what it meant to be a woman leader. Did women follow Jesus differently? How did they interact with Jesus? How did they worship him? Was there something that I was supposed to be doing?

Mary Magdalene and Mary the mother of Jesus were the most important women in Jesus's life. One is inaccurately known as a repentant prostitute, the other as a perpetual virgin.

These women are defined by whether or not they had sex. But who were they to Jesus? Did he define them by their sexual behavior too?

Mary Magdalene in particular grabbed my heart. Why had the church throughout the centuries painted her dressed in red, the color associated with seduction? Why was she seen as a sexual woman, voluptuous and tempting? In many Renaissance paintings, she looks like she is ready to lure someone to bed. Why was her sexuality so important? And why are fringe elements today trying to convince us that she really was Jesus's wife?[1]

I wanted to get to know the truth about Mary Magdalene. But where to start? My search took me all the way back to the beginning, to the creation of the human race. The role and place of women in relationship to men has been complicated from the very beginning of scripture.

In the Beginning

In the Bible, the most important stories are told more than once. The story of Jesus is told in four gospels. The story of the Exodus is told many times in the Old Testament. And the story of the creation of the world is told twice. Scripture often repeats the most crucial stories as a way of honoring and exploring them, like when we hold up a diamond and examine its many sides. Each of these stories is told from a different angle, another perspective. Sometimes the details may even conflict.

1. The most popular book that describes Mary Magdalene and Jesus as having been married is Dan Brown's *The DaVinci Code*.

For some, the existence of multiple and sometimes divergent tellings of the same story is disturbing and means that none of it really happened. For me, it makes the words more real. After all, if a story is important to me, I tell it many times and so will anyone else who witnessed it. And their story will no doubt be told from a different perspective than mine. God inspired Holy Scripture to be written not as a textbook but as a living word told in many ways from many perspectives.

So there are two creation stories. All you have to do is open the Bible and read to see that this is true. In the first of the two creation stories (found in Genesis 1–2:3), God makes the world in seven days. On each day, God calls the created good. And on the sixth day, God makes humankind. Humans, both male and female, are created *in the image of God.* They are made in God's image together. And together, God declares that they are *very good.* In the first story, man and woman are created at the same time as equals and God says that they are very good.

In the second story (found in Genesis 2:4–5), God makes a garden first and puts Adam in that garden. For centuries the translators of the Bible have used the word *Adam* as the proper name for a man, and later in the book of Genesis, this word is used as if it were the name of the man. But the word in the Hebrew is derived from the word הָאֲדָמָה (pronounced *adama*) which means "earth." So a more accurate translation of the word *Adam* might be "earth-creature" or "one made from earth." Adam is created when God takes the earth and forms it into a human shape. And God breathes into Adam the breath of life. God then sets about making some company for the earth-creature.

God creates animals, birds of the air, and fish of the sea, but still Adam is lonely. So God makes Adam go to sleep and separates Adam's *side* from the rest of his body. The result of this split is the creation of שׁיא and אִשָּׁה (*eesh* and *eesha*), male and female. These words, male and female, are different from the word Adam. So there is one earth-creature which is then split into two parts. And after the split, it seems that Adam and Eve existed in harmony and peace until the arrival of the snake.

We have only just opened the Bible and already the role and place of the woman is confusing. Was woman created alongside and equal to the man? Was she created after the splitting of an earth-creature? Who is she in relation to the man and what is her place in the created order?

These stories coexist to tell us a deep truth about who we are. The relationship between men and women is complicated and it has been from the very beginning.

Lilith and Eve

How can we understand these two different stories that sit side by side at the very beginning of the Bible? Babylonian Jewish scholars tried to make sense of the two creation stories by imagining that the woman in the first story was equal to the man and that he did not like her. They named her "the First Eve." Later, this first woman became linked with legends of a female *lilu* (demon), who stalked men in their sleep, causing nocturnal emissions. This demon also caused stillbirths and other pregnancy abnormalities. Jewish myths arose in which this first woman was called Lilith. In these myths, Lilith was banished by

Adam because she seemed too powerful, too much like him.[2] So Lilith roamed around in frustration, causing havoc in the night.

And so, the woman in the first creation story who was created right alongside and equal to the man became evil. She was banished for being proud and independent. She was blamed for unwanted sexual desire and abnormal pregnancies. Lilith was both sexual and demonic.

Meanwhile, the second story painted a very different picture of the first woman. Her name was Eve. She was subservient and submissive. In a strange twist of fate, it was Eve, the submissive woman, who became the one blamed for the fall of humanity. And it was her gender, associated with a certain kind of sexuality, which was later considered to be her method of persuasion.

Blamed for the Fall

Eve tempted Adam to eat the forbidden fruit. She ate first. She believed the lies of the snake. It was her fault that Adam fell from harmony with God. Was it because she was a woman that she made this fatal mistake? How did she convince Adam to eat? Was Adam unable to refuse because he found Eve's body so attractive? Is Eve to blame for the fall of humanity, for all of our suffering, for the fact that we have lost our place with God? *It is her fault. Isn't it?*

Did Eve use her body in convincing Adam to consume the fruit? How could she have done this if Adam himself had not yet fallen, did not realize he was naked, and felt no lust?

---

2. The only reference to "Lilith" in the Bible itself is found in Isaiah 34:14: "Wildcats shall meet with hyenas, goat-demons shall call to each other; there too Lilith shall repose, and find a place to rest."

First of all, let us go back and see exactly what the Bible says about how Eve convinced Adam to eat the fruit. Here are the simple verses from the book of Genesis.

> Now the serpent was more crafty than any other wild animal that the Lord God had made. He said to the woman, "Did God say, 'You shall not eat from any tree in the garden'?" The woman said to the serpent, "We may eat of the fruit of the trees in the garden; but God said, 'You shall not eat of the fruit of the tree that is in the middle of the garden, nor shall you touch it, or you shall die.'" But the serpent said to the woman, "You will not die; for God knows that when you eat of it your eyes will be opened, and you will be like God, knowing good and evil." So when the woman saw that the tree was good for food, and that it was a delight to the eyes, and that the tree was to be desired to make one wise, she took of its fruit and ate; and she also gave some to her husband, who was with her, and he ate.

—GENESIS 3:1–6

From this passage, scholars over the centuries created a whole universe of possibilities. Notice that Eve and the snake have a conversation but Eve never converses with Adam. Did Eve convince Adam by seducing him? Did she use her femininity as her method of persuasion? Was it all her fault?

From these simple verses of scripture, the scholar Tertullian wrote this around the year 200 AD,

> In pain shall you bring forth children, woman, and you shall turn to your husband and he shall rule over you. And do you

not know that you are Eve? God's sentence hangs still over all your sex and His punishment weighs down upon you. You are the devil's gateway; you are she who first violated the forbidden tree and broke the law of God. It was you who coaxed your way around him whom the devil had not the force to attack. With what ease you shattered that image of God: Man! Because of the death you merited, even the Son of God had to die . . . Woman, you are the gate to hell.[3]

The Book of Genesis does not say that Eve convinced Adam at all. It simply says that he was with her. How have we come to believe that he needed convincing? The words of the scripture make it sound like Adam was just there when she ate the fruit so he took a bite. There is no reference to any kind of conversation at all.

Even if Eve did convince Adam, does that make Adam and all men not responsible for the fall? Is it really all Eve's fault, all the fault of the woman? Was Adam not conscious of his own actions? This theory makes Adam seem like some kind of helpless infant, as if he were incapable of refusing Eve. Ironically, this theory gives all the power to the woman.

Even as early as the second century, the fall of humanity became associated with women. Eve was considered the most at fault because she ate the fruit first. It was her disobedience which was the focus, the root cause of the fall from Eden.

---

3. Tertullian, *On the Apparel of Women*, trans. S. Thelwall, in *Ante-Nicene Fathers*, vol. 4, ed. Alexander Roberts, James Donaldson, and A. Cleveland Coxe (Buffalo, NY: Christian Literature Publishing Co., 1885). Revised and edited for New Advent by Kevin Knight (*http://www.newadvent.org/fathers/0402.htm*).

In the second century, Clement of Alexandria wrote,

> Every woman should be filled with shame by the thought that she is a woman. . . . the consciousness of their own nature must evoke feelings of shame.
>
> —*Paedagogus* (*The Instructor*), Book 2, 33.2

Women were seen as lesser than men and this simple passage from Genesis about Eve was used to justify their reasoning. Martin Luther would later write,

> For woman seems to be a creature somewhat different from man, in that she has dissimilar members, a varied form and a mind weaker than man. Although Eve was a most excellent and beautiful creature, like unto Adam in reference to the image of God, that is with respect to righteousness, wisdom and salvation, yet she was a woman. For as the sun is more glorious than the moon, though the moon is a most glorious body, so woman, though she was a most beautiful work of God, yet she did not equal the glory of the male creature.[4]

Even earlier, about 160 AD, Justin Martyr would paint Eve as the antithesis of Mary the mother of Jesus:

> For Eve, who was a virgin and undefiled, having conceived the word of the serpent, brought forth disobedience and death. But the Virgin Mary received faith and joy, when the angel Gabriel announced the good tidings to her that the

---

4. Martin Luther, *Commentary on Genesis*, trans. John Nicolas Lenker (Gutenberg: Project Gutenberg E Books, 2015), chap. 2, pt. 5, 27b.

Spirit of the Lord would come upon her, and the power of the Highest would overshadow her.[5]

Again and again, the fall of humanity was blamed on Eve. It was the woman who was at fault. And the only way she could have convinced Adam to eat was by somehow using her body as a tool of seduction. Being a woman became a bad thing, for it was a woman who convinced Adam to eat the forbidden fruit.

Living in a Fallen World

I do believe that we live in a fallen world. Just turn on the news and watch. It is obvious. Life can seem cruel and random. When pain comes to us we feel that somehow we have been cheated. We ask God, "What have I done wrong?" Not only is pain itself difficult but it feels somehow unfair. When someone is diagnosed with an illness, they often ask, "Why is this happening to me?" They assume that they should be healthy and live always. When conflict, suffering, and even death arise, it just feels wrong. We were born assuming that life should be Eden. I believe this is evidence of the fact that we were initially created to live in Eden. We belong in Eden, in a place where there is no suffering and where we live in harmony with God. A child is born expecting and, in fact, deserving perfect care. And we parents, fallen creatures that we are, do our very best and still mess things up.

We love fairy tales for good reason. The good and the bad are so well differentiated. I love to take my boys to the movies

---

5. Justin Martyr, *Dialogue with Trypho*, ch. 100, trans. Marcus Dods and George Reith, in *Ante-Nicene Fathers*, vol. 1.

and watch the good guys beat up the bad guys. We all want to defeat evil and live happily-ever-after just like they do in the movies. It is immensely satisfying to watch because it feels right.

On some level, we still assume that life should be lived in a state of peace and joy. When I counsel young couples planning to be married, part of what I have to do is remind them that their lives will not be a happily-ever-after. No matter how good they are to each other, they will encounter pain and conflict. It is part of the fallen nature of our world. They will have to fight for their marriage. It will not be easy. And when things get difficult, it will no doubt surprise them. They will think that they have done something wrong, but really it is human nature to struggle. We just don't believe that things should be hard.

Our yearning for peace, our yearning for happiness—these are signs of the fact that we were created by God for Eden. We were designed to live in harmony with God. Eden is where we long to be; it is where things feel right. It is where we belong and we keep trying to get back there.

Humanity has fallen from paradise; there is no denying that fact. But the fall of humanity—is it the fault of the woman alone? Does she alone bear full responsibility? The man chose to eat as well, but because the woman ate first, she is considered the more fallen of the two, the great temptress.

Mary the Virgin and Mary Magdalene: The Two Extremes Continue

Echoes of Lilith and Eve were woven deeply into the Christian tradition. After Jesus's death and resurrection, when the writers of the gospels began to tell the story, there arose two import-ant women. One was Mary the mother of Jesus, the other was Mary Magdalene. In the gospels themselves, these women are portrayed with all the complexity and dimension of the men. Jesus's mother gets afraid and impatient with her son. She even tries to accuse Jesus of being possessed by a demon in order to bring him home. Mary Magdalene is a woman who has been healed by Jesus and becomes one of his most faithful followers. Jesus's relationships with both his mother and with Mary Mag-dalene seem to be relationships of mutual love and respect. It is Jesus's mother who urges him to perform his first miracle in the Gospel of John and it is Mary Magdalene who first sees the Risen Christ.

But as the centuries passed, these rich biblical characters began to be painted in black and white. Mary the mother of Jesus is described as a virgin in the gospels of Matthew and Luke. She was not yet married when she became pregnant by the Holy Spirit. Jesus did not have an earthly father, and Joseph waited until Jesus was born to have marital relations with his wife. This is an important concept, for it validates the under-standing that Jesus was born of God and of man. God was the father, humanity the mother. Over the centuries, the church began to believe that Jesus's mother Mary never had sex at all in her entire lifetime. Mary was considered a perpetual virgin.

The concept of Mary's perpetual virginity began in the sec-ond century with both Irenaeus and Origen. By the fourth cen-tury, it was well established as a teaching of the church. Mary was viewed as the second Eve, and her purity—her total lack of sexual activity during the course of her lifetime—made her

the antithesis of a temptress. John Chrysostom used the instruc-
tion of Jesus on the cross to his disciple—*behold your son, behold
your mother*—as evidence of Mary's perpetual virginity and the
fact that Jesus was her only son. Augustine of Hippo argued for
the perpetual virginity of Mary, and Thomas Aquinas argued
that to doubt the perpetual virginity of Mary was to call into
question the perfection of Christ and insult the dignity of the
Mother of God.

In the year 553, Mary was declared a perpetual virgin by
the Second Council of Constantinople. The Bible tells us that
Joseph did not know his wife sexually "until she had borne a
son" (Matthew 1:25). But this verse was overlooked. There
are also passages that refer to Jesus's brothers and sisters, but
these were translated using a secondary translation, as cousins
or friends. Even James, the brother of Jesus, was declared his
cousin.[6] It seemed essential for the church to believe that Mary
the Mother of Jesus never had sex. This is still considered an
essential doctrine in the Roman Catholic tradition today.

I have prayed to Mary myself. I find the concept of her perpetual virginity to be possible, even likely. Perhaps Mary, like
Jesus, was so in love with God that she never had sex with her
husband. In other words, perhaps the love of God replaced all
carnal desire for both of them. I do not deny that this theory is
entirely possible and would hold true with many of the saints of
the church who simply refrained from sexual activity and were

---

6. Another theory has Joseph marry another woman. This woman, called Melcha, bears
his other children and in this way, Jesus had brothers and sisters while his mother, Mary,
remained a virgin all her life.

consumed with the love of God. However, if Mary were to have sex with Joseph after the birth of Jesus, as the synoptic gospels would suggest, this would not make her less of a pure woman in my mind. To mother more children would not demean her in any way for me personally.

Hebrews 13:4 declares that marriage is honorable, including the sexual component ("the bed"). The Apostle Paul instructed the early churches that husbands and wives should not deprive or defraud one another of the sexual component of marriage (1 Corinthians 7:1–5). So why has it been so important that Jesus's mother remained a virgin for her entire life?

Would Mary, Jesus's mother, have refused to bear any other children when this was considered the joy and purpose of a woman's life? It is possible. Let me be clear that my purpose in writing these words is not to dishonor or denigrate Mary in any way. I believe that she is the greatest of the saints. If the thought of her having sex with Joseph after the birth of Jesus upsets you, please forgive me. But even if Mary did remain a virgin, why is this part of her character so much more important than all the other parts? Isn't this private between Mary and Joseph? It seems that the issue of Mary's subsequent sexual purity was of immense importance to leaders such as Pope Siricius I who wrote this in 392 AD:

> You had good reason to be horrified at the thought that another birth might issue from the same virginal womb from which Christ was born according to the flesh. For the Lord Jesus would never have chosen to be born of a virgin if he had ever judged that she would be so incontinent as to

contaminate with the seed of human intercourse the birthplace of the Lord's body, that court of the eternal king.

—LETTER TO BISHOP ANYSIUS, 392 AD

Mary the Mother of Jesus became defined by her lack of
sexual activity. It was her title. To this very day, she is called
Mary the Virgin and not Mary the Obedient or Mary the
Caretaker. We don't call Peter the One Who Had Sex or John
the Virgin. I can understand why Mary's virginity was vitally
important in the birth of Jesus, but why would it remain so
for the rest of her lifetime? Why is it so important whether
or not Jesus's mother ever had sex? I wonder why her sexual
activity, or lack of, has to become such a central part of her
identity. Is sex really that important? Would Mary the Mother
of Jesus have been less pure if she had sexual relations with
her husband after the birth of Jesus? Why do we let her sexual
behavior define her whole life? Is sex really that important?

In the Eastern Orthodox tradition, Jesus's mother became
known by another title. Rather than the Blessed Virgin Mary,
Mary is called *Theotokos* in the Eastern Church. The word means
God-bearer, the one who carried God in her womb. This concept
of God-bearer is much more active than the concept of perpetual virgin. Instead of focusing on what Mary does not do, this
concept of God-bearer focuses on what Mary was able to accom-
plish by literally hosting God within her womb. It means that
Mary must have been immensely strong, powerful, pure, and
attractive all at the same time. A mother is the ultimate protector
and benefactor of the child within her. There is no higher honor
than to protect and provide for God Almighty. The power of this

theological concept can be immensely liberating for all women. This was our most powerful role in biblical times, the one thing that the men could never do. Women could bear and sustain life. And Mary bore God's life. She was strong enough to carry God within her.

In the beginning of the fifth century, John Cassian wrote,

> You cannot then help admitting that the grace comes from God. It is God, then, who has given it. But it has been given by our Lord Jesus Christ. Therefore the Lord Jesus Christ is God. But if he is God, as he certainly is, then she who bore God is the Mother of God.
>
> —On the Incarnation of Christ Against Nestorius 2:2 (429 AD)

Mary was and is the Mother of God. Isn't that much more important than whether or not she had sex with her husband after Jesus was born? Should we not define Mary by what she accomplished rather than what she refrained to do? Should we not refer to her as mother, as God-bearer, rather than as perpetual virgin?

At the same time that Jesus's mother was being defined by her sexual activity, Mary Magdalene was also being reinvented. But Magdalene was cast as the opposite extreme. She was rapidly becoming known as a prostitute.

2

Sex on the Brain

Lord, make me chaste, but not yet.
—St. Augustine, Confessions

The feminine body, sex, and original sin were all wrapped together into a nice package by the brilliant theologian St. Augustine in the fourth century. Augustine was convinced that God wanted him to renounce his plans for marriage and remain celibate. And there was the rub, for Augustine found himself trapped and unable at first to live a celibate life. Here was a man with an immense sexual drive who was trying to live like a monk. Rather than becoming married and expressing all his desire with his wife in a socially acceptable context, Augustine believed that the only true path to God was to refrain from all sexual activity. Augustine had a mistress for many years and she even bore him a son. But his decision to become a Christian and later a priest meant that he had to send her away. For Augustine, there was no temptation greater than the temptation to have sex.

In Augustine's *Confessions* (book 6, chapters 7–16), he struggles to reign in his desire to love a woman physically. He lived with an unnamed concubine for years in a monogamous relationship, but in order to grow closer to God, Augustine felt it necessary to send her away so that he could live his life as a celibate. Augustine was convinced that he could not know God fully if he was having sex with a woman.

For Augustine, lust was the opposite of faithfulness. He wrote in his confessions,

> So these two wills within me, one old, one new, one the servant of the flesh, the other of the spirit, were in conflict and between them they tore my soul apart. (VIII.5.1)

In book 8 of the *Confessions*, Augustine described how trapped he felt by his own desire. After his concubine was dismissed, he found himself behaving promiscuously. Here he describes his situation, sounding as though he suffered from some kind of sexual addiction.

> I was bound not by an iron imposed by anyone else but by the iron of my own choice. The enemy had a grip on my will and so made a chain for me to hold me a prisoner. The consequence of a distorted will is passion. By servitude to passion, habit is formed, and habit to which there is no resistance becomes a compulsion. By these links, as it were, connected one to another (hence my term a chain), a harsh bondage held me under restraint.[1]

Augustine was not able to give up his sexual activity at first. His desire for sex had become the point of his resistance to the

---

1. Saint Augustine of Hippo, *Confessions*, Book VIII (Harmondsworth, Middlesex, England: Penguin Books, 1961).

will of God. Augustine became convinced that lust and desire were tools of the devil. And as a consequence, the female body became the instrument of temptation.

Augustine was able to articulate the fact that lust seemed to cloud his judgment and prevent him from acting rationally. Lust was a carnal temptation that drew him away from God.

> Bodily desire, like a morass, and adolescent sex welling up within me exuded mists which clouded over and obscured my heart, so that I could not distinguish the clear light of true love from the murk of lust. (II.2.1)

Augustine saw his lust as the opposite of his intention to pray. Lust was not just carnal for Augustine, it was evil, for it drew him away from God's purpose for his life. Augustine believed that the will of the flesh had the power to tear his soul apart. He gave lust and sexual matters an immense power, the power to drag his soul into hell. He saw all forms of sex or sexual desire leading to hell. For Augustine, a man could not be devout and faithful and sexually active, even within the confines of marriage.

If sex is seen as dangerous to the soul, then the woman's body can be seen as an agent of destruction, a tool for the seduction of the soul to hell. Except for their role in bearing children, it would be better if women simply did not exist. Her body, according to Augustine, gives rise to lust in the man and lust deters the man from his faithfulness to God.

Augustine did not believe that a woman, on her own, was made in the image of God. He wrote,

Woman was merely man's helpmate, a function which pertains to her alone. She is not the image of God but as far as man is concerned, he is by himself the image of God.

—DE TRINITATE, 12-7-10

Here is what he thought of women:

Women should not be enlightened or educated in any way. They should, in fact, be segregated as they are the cause of hideous and involuntary erections in holy men.[2]

Women, according to Augustine, were the cause of erections in men. It was the fault of their bodies. The woman's body was nothing more than an agent of temptation.

Sex and Society

Augustine was a brilliant writer. His words have echoed through the centuries, influencing Western Christianity. Like Augustine, Western culture has become obsessed with sex. We are obsessed with sex even today. While the world is torn by poverty and war, much of the Western Protestant Church finds itself embroiled in controversy about sex and sexuality. In most recent times, in the United States, entire denominations have split over views on sexual orientation and gay marriage. Matters of sex and sexuality have taken on a massive status, rivaling the divinity of Christ or belief in the Trinity. For some reason, we cannot worship with people who think differently than we do on matters of sex.

---

2. Quoted from St. Augustine, in Christopher Reyes, *In His Name*, vol. 4 (Bloomington, IN: Trafford Publishing, 2014), 368.

Jesus never mentions sex explicitly in the gospels, but he talks about money all the time. What if we talked about money and generosity instead of sex? I remind my congregation of this fact a lot, and it seems to quiet the discussion down immediately!

How is it that we have become so obsessed with sex? Did this fascination begin when we jumped on the bandwagon with Augustine and began to believe that sex was linked with the devil? St. Paul advises that a person with sexual desire marry and devote themselves to their spouse. Sexual desire within the context of marriage is good. Why not simply encourage all people to find this commitment joyful and move on? Fascination with lust only creates more obsession. I pray that there will come a time when we don't have to make sex and sexual attraction the central and defining part of our character.

Shame

What happens when the female body is seen as tempting men to do evil? The woman becomes unnaturally absorbed with her body, how she looks, how attractive she is. Her body becomes a source of power but also a source of shame. The woman becomes obsessed with her body. In a world where men possess power, intelligent women cannot help but notice that they can use their bodies to gain favor with men. And hence they begin to pay undue attention to the upkeep and care of their bodies. The attractive woman can influence men more than the ugly woman. And women needed all the help they could get.

By connecting original sin with sex, St. Augustine lit the fire of an obsession that had been brewing for centuries. Certainly the concept of sex and the female body was present all throughout scripture, but Augustine forever wed sex with an understanding of the fall of humanity. Augustine made sex dangerous and fascinating at the same time. And since Augustine, western culture has become entangled in a web of fascination and shame when it comes to the female body. Women today are obsessed with their bodies. We are never satisfied. I watch my weight like a hawk. The first thing I do in the morning is hop on a scale and look in the mirror. What if I opened my Bible instead? What if I looked at an icon or painting or at God's creation outside instead of looking in the mirror? Or better yet, what if I learned to love the body that God has given to me? What if I woke up to thank God for every inch of my physical being, no matter what its appearance or function? Women must work both mentally and physically to counteract the cultural forces that would have us judge our bodies. Activities like yoga, massage, or simply meditating on the gift of the body are ways to begin. We have much work to do in this area as women.[3]

As a priest, I often see young women who feel depressed because they hate their bodies. And why wouldn't they, when our advertisements promote girls who are so thin that they may be bordering on anorexic? How could anyone love their body in

---

3. "The story has timeless appeal, first, because that problem of 'how'—whether love should be eros or agape; sensual or spiritual; a matter of longing or consummation—defines the human condition. What makes the conflict universal is the dual experience of sex: the necessary means of reproduction and the madness of passionate encounter. For women, the maternal can seem to be at odds with the erotic, a tension that in men can be reduced to the well-known opposite fantasies of the madonna and the whore." Read more: *http://www. smithsonianmag.com/history/who-was-mary-magdalene-119565482/#xuSVG9EfmCVgp6Ib .99; article by James Carroll.*

this environment? We have shamed the female body and made it an object to be scrutinized rather than a living gift, part of God's beloved creation. What woman has not grabbed the fat around her hips and belly and wished she could just get it off? Rather than marveling at how our eyes can see and our ears can hear, we slap our cellulite and pinch our bellies. We are ashamed of our bodies. We must think and pray about ways to counteract these cultural impulses to hatred and judgment when it comes to our bodies. How can we teach our young women to love their physical selves?

In his book, *The Soul of Shame*, Curt Thompson writes, "Shame interferes with good listening at every level and every opportunity. . . . In this way, shame is a shared process whose mission is to disrupt connection between people."[4] When a person feels shame, it separates that person from the essence of who they were created to be. If we return to the creation story in the book of Genesis, notice how both Adam and Eve hid when they realized that they were naked. They felt ashamed. Shame causes us to run from God and from one another. It is shame, not sex, that is the first and most primal response to the fall of humanity. Shame separates us from God, from each other, and from our true selves. When we feel ashamed, we run from God and we hide our true selves.

We have shamed Mary Magdalene, and as a result, we have not listened to her story. Through the centuries, and even up to the present day, we have told stories about her sexual activity as

---

4. Curt Thompson, *The Soul of Shame: Retelling the Stories We Believe about Ourselves* (Downers Grove, IL: Intervarsity Press, 2015), 89.

if it was the most important part of who she was. When Dan Brown published his bestseller *The Da Vinci Code*, it was just another step on this path of obsession with Mary Magdalene's sex life. Brown wrote that Mary Magdalene not only had sex with Jesus but married him and they had children. Of course, we find no mention of this within the canonical gospels, but in a culture obsessed with sex, we find ourselves fascinated by the thought of Jesus's sex life. And who better for Jesus to sleep with than Mary Magdalene? After all, she was a prostitute, right? Imagining that Jesus of Nazareth and Mary Magdalene could have loved one another as master and disciple seems impossible to us, too dry, too boring. We must inject sex to continue our obsession. Simple love of God and simple devotion . . . well, it's just too bland for a sex-crazed culture.

By cloaking Mary Magdalene in sex and shame, we have effectively silenced her. We have lost the witness of one of the greatest followers of Jesus. Let us take off this mantle of shame and uncover who she really was. But first, we must finish clarifying who she was not.

3

⌒

The Real Mary

In Jesus's day, a woman was valued according to how many children she produced. The word for woman in the ancient Greek of the Gospels is γυνή. It means life-bearer, the bearer of children, a walking womb of sorts. Women were vessels for the purpose of bearing children. They were considered property to be owned by their husband, father, or closest male relative. They were valued for their wombs, for the only thing that women could do and men could not—for the bearing and nursing of children, particularly sons. Women such as Hannah, Sarai, and Rachel found their value only in having children. They were lost until God granted them the gift of a child.

Women often wore their heads covered just as many do in the Middle East today. A woman's face and her body were covered not only because of the heat but because each woman belonged to her husband or father. She was not to be looked at by other men.

Women who cover their bodies and heads all look alike. And once they look alike, men begin to believe that they *are* all alike. Why would it be important to distinguish one woman from another when women were not to be noticed outside of their husbands and immediate families? It became easy for men to fall prey to the illusion that all women were the same. Just as black slaves were often viewed not as individuals but as many copies of one lesser species, just as Jews during the Holocaust were not seen as individual human beings, so women were lumped into one single female. Individuality would have only threatened the system and encouraged relationships. Better to see all women as one. Women were property, vessels for the purpose of having children. Don't look at their faces or their eyes too closely. No wonder Mary Magdalene was confused with other women.

For hundreds of years, Mary Magdalene has been lumped together with two other women who played roles in Jesus's life. Let's look at these biblical passages that have caused so much confusion about Mary Magdalene.

At the beginning of the seventh century, Pope Gregory the Great would solidify the misconception that Mary Magdalene was the sinner with the alabaster jar. Gregory was raised in the Roman nobility and had been assigned as a prefect to Rome. When his father died, Gregory became a monk. He turned his Roman mansion into a monastery where he became an expert in repentance and discipline. The plague was sweeping across Europe and Gregory taught that one must battle the plague with acts of penitence and severe discipline. Refraining from sex and the association of women was chief among those acts of penitence. When the previous Pope died of the plague, Gregory was made Pope and he taught that one must pray, fast, give alms, and stay the heck away from women if one were to prevent the plague. He did not blame the plague itself directly on women, but he believed that women led to temptation which led to God's wrath in the form of the plague. Here is what Pope Gregory preached about Mary Magdalene,

> She whom Luke calls the sinful woman, whom John calls Mary, we believe to be the Mary from whom seven devils were ejected according to Mark. What did these seven devils signify, if not all the vices?
>
> It is clear, that the woman previously used the unguent to perfume her flesh in forbidden acts. What she therefore displayed more scandalously, she was now offering to God in a more praiseworthy manner. She had coveted with earthly eyes, but now through penitence these are consumed with tears. She displayed her hair to set off her face, but now her hair dries her tears. She had spoken proud things with her mouth, but in kissing the Lord's feet, she now planted her mouth on the Redeemer's feet. For every delight, therefore, she had had in herself, she now immolated herself. She turned the mass of her crimes to virtues, in order to serve God entirely in penance.
>
> —POPE GREGORY THE GREAT (HOMILY XXXIII)[1]

Pope Gregory talks about "the mass of her crimes." But what crimes did Mary Magdalene actually commit? All that we know of her tells us that she was tormented with demons. So why did the church, for centuries and centuries, believe that she was

---

1. *https://en.wikipedia.org/wiki/Mary_Magdalene#cite_note-Smithsonian-28.*

such a sinner? Why did we have to shame Mary Magdalene for so long?

The Woman with Oil

Pope Gregory the Great believed that Mary Magdalene was the woman who anointed Jesus's feet with perfume and wiped them with her hair. In all four gospels, there is a story of such a woman. This woman pours costly oil over Jesus, but in no account does the writer of the gospel mention that her name was Mary Magdalene.

In Matthew, Mark, and Luke, the woman with the oil is not named. She simply enters the house and begins to anoint Jesus. In Matthew and Mark, she anoints Jesus's head as one would anoint a king. In Luke, she anoints Jesus's feet and wipes them with her hair, crying all the while. Only in Luke is the woman called "a sinner." She is described as ἁμαρτωλός, which simply means sinner, not anything necessarily sexual in nature.

In the Gospel of John, the woman is identified as Mary of Bethany, the sister of Martha and Lazarus. Mary of Bethany hosted Jesus with her sister and brother in the small village of Bethany just outside Jerusalem. Mary of Bethany never traveled with Jesus and did not have demons. She was an entirely different person from Mary Magdalene.

When Jesus heals an unnamed man, scholars do not conflate that man with one of the disciples. They just assume that a man came to Jesus for healing. So why do we assume that the woman who anointed Jesus was Mary Magdalene? There is absolutely no evidence that Mary Magdalene anointed Jesus in this way.

But women were not treated as individuals in the time of the writing of the gospels. It was easy to lump women together into one person. No one noticed the differences between them.

The Woman Caught in Adultery

Mary Magdalene is never described as a prostitute in the gospels. The word πόρνη (*porne*), which is often translated as prostitute, was also a much larger word that could refer to anyone who had sex outside of marriage. It was not necessary for a person to be paid for sex to be called πόρνη (we get the word pornography from this ancient Greek word). But again, *not once is Mary Magdalene described using this word.* So how in the world did Mary Magdalene become known as a prostitute for hundreds of years? Perhaps Mary became known as a prostitute when she became confused, yet again, with another woman: the woman who was caught in adultery.

> The scribes and the Pharisees brought a woman who had been caught in adultery; and making her stand before all of them, they said to him, "Teacher, this woman was caught in the very act of committing adultery. Now in the law Moses commanded us to stone such women. Now what do you say?"
>
> —JOHN 8:3–5

The woman who is brought before Jesus for punishment because of her adultery is never named. She is made to stand before the crowd in shame. She is not given a voice. We do not know if she was raped or if she actually approached another woman's husband. We know nothing about her. A married woman who had sex with another man was blamed even if the other man attacked her. She was soiled because no one could tell who the father of the baby was. If she became pregnant, and thus made physical evidence of her crime, she could be killed.

If this adulterous woman had been Mary Magdalene, surely the gospel writer would have mentioned that fact. Especially since Mary Magdalene will later take on such a pivotal role in the resurrection story. If she was traveling with Jesus, this crime would have been even more unlikely. How could she have committed adultery when she was spending all her time ministering to Jesus?

Why the Prostitute?

On the western shore of the Sea of Galilee, the town of Magdala was near Tiberias and was home to many Gentiles and Samaritans.[2] Because of the large number of non-Jews, the town was considered defiled by faithful Jews. Magdala was a city of some wealth and commerce. According to the Talmud, Magdala was a town of prosperity and was eventually destroyed by the Romans because of its moral depravity. The historian Flavius Josephus wrote of a town that he called Tarichea located at the exact same spot as Magdala. Josephus, a Jewish historian, also describes Tarichea as being destroyed by the Romans for its moral corruption. Before its destruction, Josephus describes the city as

---

2. Richard Losch, *The Uttermost Part of the Earth: A Guide to Places in the Bible* (Grand Rapids, MI: Wm. B. Eerdmans Publishing, 2005), 132.

having 40,000 people, a fleet of 230 boats, and a hippodrome.[3] This would have been about the year 66 CE.

Mary Magdalene must have been assumed to be a prostitute because she hailed from a city renowned for its party life.[4] There is no evidence of her acting as a prostitute, however. Certainly just because a person hails from a city that has a reputation does not mean that everyone in that city behaves in the same manner: not everyone who lives in Las Vegas is a gambler, nor does everyone who lives in Maine catch lobsters.

The truth is that a woman who was possessed by demons would have been a total outcast. She may have been raped but no one would have paid her for sex, nor would she have had the capacity to collect money for her favors. Demoniacs lived outside the towns among the tombs. They were considered dangerous and frightening. Mary Magdalene would not have been married. If she had family to care for her, she would have been very fortunate. She probably survived alone, a very sick woman just trying to stay alive.

As I mentioned before, there is a word for sinner in the ancient language of the gospels, but there is no specific word for prostitute. Mary hailed from a city that had prostitution as well as many other practiced vices, but that city was large and housed many women who were married or chaste. How did Mary become known as a prostitute when there is not even a

---

3. Watson E. Mills and Roger Aubrey Bullard, *Mercer Dictionary of the Bible* (Macon, GA: Mercer University Press, 1990), 539.

4. Writes Losch, "From early times, tradition has identified her as a prostitute possibly because of the reputation of Magdala as a depraved place. Again, this is neither affirmed nor denied in the Bible" (*The Uttermost Part of the Earth*, 132).

word for prostitute in the gospels? Perhaps simply by hailing from such a city and being single meant that men assumed she created a business for herself, surviving by using her body to make money for sex. But Mary would have been unable to live such a lifestyle, given her many ailments. Why did people throughout history just assume she was a woman who sold her body? Maybe we needed the two female archetypes—the good and the bad, the pure and the dirty, the virgin and the prostitute—in order to express a deep and abiding confusion over the role and place of women, a confusion that has been part of Western culture for thousands of years.

Even today, I can see the struggle between the images of virgin and prostitute in young women. When I talk to girls in my church, they tell me that they want to be sexy and desirable and yet innocent and pure. They want to seem experienced and have men chasing them but they don't want to appear "like a whore." They are torn between two impossible extremes and they don't know who to become.

Another Mary

Rather than picturing Mary Magdalene as a prostitute, I have another image in mind. I believe that Mary Magdalene was much more like the woman who sits outside the cathedral where I serve. Her name is Candy, and she is homeless. Candy has been diagnosed by the medical facility at our local homeless shelter. They tell me that she is a paranoid schizophrenic. When Candy is on her medications, she sits quietly and talks to her hand. When she is not on her medications, she is screaming at things we cannot see. Her screams are frightening. She does not let me get close to her. She yells obscenities and cries out for her life. It is so hard to help her. She hates to be inside. She hates to take medication. Her face is constantly sunburned. We clothe her and feed her with our shelters and clothing programs, but she wanders the streets, red-faced and screaming obscenities. Like Mary Magdalene, Candy is in bondage.

If you go to the urban core of any city, you are likely to find someone like Mary Magdalene, lost and on the streets, raped, afraid to be near anyone. Candy gravitates to the area around our cathedral. I often see her sitting nearby, but she won't let me near her. "Stay away from me!" she screams. "Just stay away!"

Mary Magdalene was tormented by things that she could not see. We do not know how she got these demons, just as I don't know how Candy became so ill. I know an amazing woman who works with mentally ill people on the streets here in Jacksonville. She once explained to me that paranoid schizophrenia often comes about when a child is raped at an early age. It is as if the soul of a person is ripped by the violence and into that gap darkness enters. But I am getting ahead of myself. Let's look at what the writers of the gospels meant when they talked about demons.

4

Demons

Soon afterwards he went on through cities and villages, pro-
claiming and bringing the good news of the kingdom of God.
The twelve were with him, as well as some women who had
been cured of evil spirits and infirmities: Mary, called Magdalene, from whom seven demons had gone out, and Joanna, the
wife of Herod's steward Chuza, and Susanna, and many others,
who provided for them out of their resources.

—LUKE 8:1–3

According to the writers of both Luke and Mark, Mary
Magdalene was possessed by seven demons. How are we to
understand what this means to us today? What does it mean to
be possessed by demons?

The Unseen World

I am a priest, not a scientist. But even I know that something
is going on in the world of quantum physics. When Einstein
conceived of his theory of relativity, he opened our consciousness to the possibility of many dimensions, most of which we

cannot see. Einstein taught us that light behaved in ways that we could not comprehend or rationalize. The universe became a mysterious place of many dimensions that exist far beyond our perception.

Whether as enemies or friends, science and religion have always influenced one another. Our concept of God grows as we discover more about the universe, or as God reveals more about the universe to us. Sir Isaac Newton and others introduced us to the scientific reason of proving a hypothesis. If something behaved demonstrably in a particular way in our visible world, then we had proven the hypothesis was correct. This kind of scientific reasoning even began to influence the way that we studied the Bible. Biblical scholars began trying to prove or disprove the events of the Bible. A new field called biblical criticism was born. The idea was that one could prove what occurred in the Bible based on rational observation. At its height, the biblical criticism movement produced the Jesus Seminar, where scholars attempted to determine what Jesus did and said. The criteria for determining the truth was based solely on what the human eye could see and what could be proven by the basic laws of nature. Much of what the gospels portray as Jesus's words and actions were considered to be folklore. All exorcisms were cast aside as improbable with very little explanation. The Jesus Seminar excluded so much of the gospels that they determined the only words Jesus might have said in the Lord's Prayer were "Abba" and "Give us this day our daily bread."

But science is bringing us to a new place today. We are beginning to open our minds to realize that there is much that we cannot see or prove but that does, in fact, exist. We now conceive of a universe full of forces that move and act beyond the range of the human eye. We are beginning to glimpse the limits of our mental capabilities as well as our physical perception.

When I was in divinity school at Yale, I came to know a biology professor. Professor Evelyn Hutchinson was the winner of the Kyoto Prize, the equivalent of a Nobel Prize in biology. He was in his nineties, bent over from osteoporosis, but had eyes as bright and lively as those of a child. Every Sunday, he went to church and would kneel at the altar rail to take communion, his frail body bending low before the cross. Professor Hutchinson once asked me if I was going to preach about the scripture. When I said yes, he told me that, if he had to preach a sermon about the Bible, he would have to get up in the pulpit and just shrug his shoulders. "After all," he said, "we know so little about God."

For many years, those who considered themselves intellectuals dismissed the notion of demons and of angels. These concepts were considered superstitions and old-fashioned, the stuff of the developing world, a sign of primitive civilizations. This can be true no longer. It is time for the world of science and the world of faith to turn back towards one another. To study the workings of the universe is a form of reverence. There is no reason why a person cannot believe in the basic tenets of the Bible and embrace science at the same time. The world of quantum physics has returned us to mystery itself. We are once again humbled before the grandeur of the universe.

In order to unveil who Mary Magdalene truly was, we must take seriously the concept of demons. Mary was possessed and this experience made her who she was. We will not be able to understand the full nature of Mary's character and the remarkable relationship that she had with Jesus if we do not take seriously the possibility that there are such things as demons, unclean spirits, angels, and other forces we cannot see but that nevertheless exist and influence every one of us.

Demons in the Gospels

There is no denying that the exorcism of demons was a significant part of Jesus's ministry. The word δαίμων is used 53 times in the gospels. The Gospel of Mark is considered the earliest of the four gospels. Mark mentions Satan or the casting out of demons thirteen times. Matthew mentions Jesus exorcising demons in many people immediately after his temptation in the desert and before the Sermon on the Mount. John describes the reason for the coming of the Son of God in this way, "The Son of God was revealed for this purpose, to destroy the works of the devil" (1 John 3:8).

Jesus healed. Jesus taught. Jesus cast out demons. All of these aspects of Jesus's ministry on earth should be taken seriously and reflected upon. About one-fifth of the gospels record Jesus's healing miracles, 727 of the 3779 verses across the four gospels. Of the thirty-one miracles that Jesus performs, nine of them involve the casting out of a demon or demons. Clearly exorcism was an important part of Jesus's ministry. We could not remove the thread of exorcisms from the synoptic gospels without tearing at the fabric of the narratives themselves.

A person of faith must determine how to interpret all of scripture as a whole. How can we take literally language of the New Testament about a Holy Spirit (*pneuma hagion*) and to ignore the language referring to an unclean spirit (*pneuma akatharta*)? If we are to embrace the power of the Holy Spirit which we cannot see, then we must also take seriously the existence of the unclean spirits and demons that clearly impacted Jesus's life and ministry.

Let us unpack this thought for a moment, namely that a believer who embraces the concept of the Holy Spirit must also consider the reality of unclean spirits. If we are to open ourselves to the mystery of an unseen presence of God that can influence, heal, and change our lives, then it is inconsistent to write off all other kinds of unseen influences. Jesus spends a lot of time casting out spirits that no one could see. Was this aspect of his ministry pretend? Are the unclean spirits that existed back then simply no longer present today? At the very least, every Christian must pray and consider the fact that demons existed in Jesus's day and it is more than likely that they exist today as well, we just call them by another name.

Language

It is important to remember that the lexicon of Aramaic and the Greek spoken in Jesus's day was significantly smaller than that of our modern English. When we translate the Bible from its ancient languages into English, we must take a big, roomy word that carried a wide range of meanings and select among more specific, precise, narrow English words. There are approximately one million words in current American English usage; the New Testament contains 140,000 Greek words. That means that the

Greek of the New Testament utilizes only fourteen percent of our language. Or, to be more precise, the entire meaning of the New Testament must be conveyed by choosing only fourteen percent of our words. Every time we translate scripture, we take a large, expansive word and choose among smaller, more precise English words. Every time we translate, *we limit meaning.*

The word δαίμον (*diamon*) in the gospels was a big word. It was an umbrella, covering many things. Demon was a word used for anything that seemed to take over a person and that could not be explained. Demons could range from what we would identify now as physical ailments, such as epilepsy, to what we would now understand to be mental health issues such as schizophrenia, anorexia, or bulimia. Demons also represented spiritual torture and bondage of a nature that is still a mystery today. Demon referred to an unseen reality: Whenever a person acted in ways that made no sense, they were considered to be possessed by a demon. Demons radically altered a person's behavior. They could force a person to do embarrassing things, to expose themselves or drool or scream. Demons caused people to faint, writhe on the ground and foam at the mouth, talk to those unseen, or behave in other disturbing ways. The word demon was used to point to something unwanted and scary, an invisible enemy, possessing and changing a person into someone that they did not want to become.

Everything from seizures, to incessant weeping, to cutting oneself, to screaming at nothing, to talking gibberish . . . all of these behaviors were simply called demons. Demons took over a person and caused them to act in irrational ways. They were scary and they could be deadly. Today we have a myriad of ways of explaining these kinds of behaviors. We use the language of psychiatry, medicine, and other disciplines. These words are much more precise but they are also sanitary, they do not touch the spiritual aspect of these ailments. Meanwhile, the word demon has been relegated to horror movies. Mainstream Americans think that the word demon belongs in fairytales or the Middle Ages. We have removed the word demon from our vocabulary. We have ignored the very real spiritual dimension of these battles of the mind and body. And wouldn't demons want that? For if the scripture is true, the last thing that a demon wants is to be brought into the light.

Exorcisms: How Did Jesus Do It?

The exorcism of Mary Magdalene is not described in the gospels. All that we know is that Jesus cast seven demons out of Mary Magdalene. In order to understand how Jesus cast out demons, it might helpful for us to turn to a passage from Luke where an exorcism is described in greater detail.

> In the synagogue there was a man who had the spirit of an unclean demon, and he cried out with a loud voice, "Let us alone! What have you to do with us, Jesus of Nazareth? Have you come to destroy us? I know who you are, the Holy One of God." But Jesus rebuked him, saying, "Be silent, and come out of him!" When the demon had thrown him down before them, he came out of him without having done him any harm.
>
> —LUKE 4:33–35

In this telling, the first and perhaps most important thing that occurred was the identification of the demons. Demons spoke directly to Jesus and immediately identified themselves. Jesus's presence itself seemed to bring out the unclean spirits, to force them to self-identify. Many of the demoniacs that Jesus healed had been possessed for years. No one had been able to bring the demon out. The demons seemed to want to hide inside a person, tormenting them. But the mere presence of Jesus seemed to force the demon into the light. There was no hiding in the presence of Jesus.

Demons seemed to recognize who Jesus was when no one else did. In this case, the demon speaks through the man, yelling in an agitated state. In all of the exorcisms, Jesus addresses the demon directly and curtly with a command. He does not converse. He does not even pray. He simply tells the demon to leave. Speaking directly to the entity, Jesus uses short, powerful words and commands it to depart. He does not even use the name of God. Jesus just orders the demon to leave.

As opposed to the healings, Jesus never touches a demoniac. He uses only words of command. In this case, he simply silences the demon and tells it to leave.

Jesus never engages in conversation with a demon. Later, when Jesus gives his disciples the authority to cast out demons in his name, they will also command demons to leave, this time in Jesus's name, but will not converse with the demon or even answer its questions.

Using this story from Luke's gospel as our model, there appear to be three rather straightforward steps to each exorcism.

1. Identify the unclean spirit.
2. Do not confuse the unclean spirit with the one it possesses.
3. Command it to leave, no more and no less.

We can only assume that Jesus exorcised Mary Magdalene in just the same way: by identifying her demons, having compassion on her but not touching her, and commanding the demons to leave. As with the other exorcisms, Mary was most likely healed quickly, with no fanfare or applause. In a few moments, her life of torment was changed forever.

5

Saintly Struggles

I do not understand my own actions. For I do not do what I want, but I do the very thing I hate. Now if I do what I do not want, I agree that the law is good. But in fact it is no longer I that do it, but sin that dwells within me.

—PAUL, IN ROMANS 7:15–17

If you understand the nighttime sky, you understand how the stars' positions change. Not to understand those patterns of change is not to understand the sky. The mind changes too.

—DAVID GELERNTER, *THE TIDES OF MIND*[1]

In the early 1500s, Ignatius of Loyola created a new form of meditation. Later called the Ignatian exercises, the meditations instructed Christians to study the Bible by imagining that they were inside the stories. With whom do you identify in the story? Pick a saint, and go inside his or her skin. Become that person, much like an actor would become the character that she portrayed. Ignatius believed that we could come to know Jesus

1. David Gelernter, *The Tides of Mind: Uncovering the Spectrum of Consciousness* (New York: Liveright, 2016), 2.

of Nazareth on a deeper level if we pictured ourselves walking alongside him as one of his followers.

To enter the story of Mary Magdalene is to enter a world of the mind, where demons tormented her and healing took place. If we are to understand her character and her relationship with Jesus, we have to consider how her mind worked; such efforts will eventually lead us to consider how our own minds work.

How do we understand the human mind? Sigmund Freud spent his life trying to explain the workings of the human mind, a pioneer in unexplored territory. His writings have deeply affected modern therapy. But Sigmund Freud saw religion and religious devotion as a form of neurosis. He wrote,

> Religion is an attempt to get control over the sensory world, in which we are placed, by means of the wish-world, which we have developed inside us as a result of biological and psychological necessities. . . . If one attempts to assign to religion its place in man's evolution, it seems not so much to be a lasting acquisition, as a parallel to the neurosis which the civilized individual must pass through on his way from childhood to maturity.[2]

Freud believed that a mature person must leave all belief behind.

As a result of Freud's teaching, a divorce occurred between the mental health profession and faith communities. Many psychoanalysts viewed religion as a crutch to be studied, not a source of healing. To this day, there are mental health

---

2. Sigmund Freud, *From Moses to Monotheism* (New York: Alfred A. Knopf, 1939).

professionals who view faith in a negative light. Many therapists have neglected to take the spiritual into full consideration.

On the other side of the divorce, people of faith who go willingly to a medical doctor when they injure their bodies consider the only option for depression, anxiety, or other mental ailments to be more and "harder" prayer. As a priest, I often attempt to convince people that God works through therapists, medication, and other treatments, that, in fact, therapy can be an answer to prayer. Why would God not utilize all the tools at our disposal? Why would God not heal through the research, medicine, and therapy that humans have worked so hard to develop? Are these forms of treatment not also valid paths to the healing grace of God?

Mary Magdalene, as a saint of the church, can serve as a bridge between the mental health discipline and the faith community. Here was a woman who suffered from spiritual, medical, and psychological ailments. Mary Magdalene models for us how to pursue both mental and spiritual health.

Demons and Dangerous Talk

I have led retreats and workshops on demons and the human mind for almost a decade. I believe that we need to reenter the language of scripture when grappling with the complexity of our own minds. The medical and psychological language that we use is simply too sanitary; it does not capture the spiritual aspect of many mental health struggles. At the same time, by venturing into the language of scripture, we run great risks. The language of demons lends itself to a potent and even dangerous kind of judgment.

I have seen people use the word demon to judge another human being, to cast that person aside or refuse to engage with them. A demon in scripture is a tempter and does not make the demoniac evil. The person remains a child of God, a child of God who has been powerfully influenced, or even possessed, by destructive thoughts and feelings. It is essential that we understand the depth and complexity of the New Testament understanding of demon if we are to use this word. It is not a word of condemnation, no the word demon is an attempt to identify a force of destruction that can live within a person. Again, the person itself is not to be judged. However, their behavior is to be judged.

So how do we take these matters seriously and examine our own minds from a spiritual perspective and yet not fall victim to calling everything bad demonic? Who has the right to name a demon? And who can cast out a demon?

As we've already noted, the writers of the gospels talk at some length about demons. Luke tells us that demons can leave a person, and then sometimes return in greater force than before.

> When the unclean spirit has gone out of a person, it wanders through waterless regions looking for a resting place, but not finding any, it says, "I will return to my house from which I came." When it comes, it finds it swept and put in order. Then it goes and brings seven other spirits more evil than itself, and they enter and live there; and the last state of that person is worse than the first.
>
> —Luke 11:24–26

After Mary's healing, she stayed well. Not once do the gospels mention that she entertained demons again. Even when Jesus was suffering on the cross, she does not return to her old tormentors. How did she stay well?

Luke's gospel passage tells us that we must fill the empty spaces of our minds once an unclean thought or spirit has departed. Mary filled her mind with devotion for Jesus. She walked with him, prayed with him, listened to his teaching, cleaned and cooked for him. She pursued Jesus with vigor and filled every inch of her mind with love and adoration for him. If the demons did try to return to her mind, they found no place to enter. Father Richard Rohr suggests that one who has been possessed by an addiction or a demon must become repossessed by God. Only God can fill the empty space where the demon once resided. Rohr writes,

> The ancients were not as naïve as we might think. In these stories, we see exactly what internalization of negative values means. . . . In general, the only cure for negative possession is a positive re-possession! Jesus is always "repossessing people"—for themselves and for God.[3]

In these modern days of fast fixes, the simple practice of the Christian faith looks dull. But there is no better aid in making a person well and whole than the simple, repetitive, and even demanding practices of the faith. And these are three-fold.

---

3. Richard Rohr, *Things Hidden: Scripture as Spirituality* (London: SPCK, 2016), 112.

1. **Each of us must pray to God every day.** If your mind races around like a monkey (that is normal as we exist in an over-stimulated culture), try walking and praying, cleaning and praying, yoga, painting, singing, or other forms of movement. But leave space for God to enter. Try reading Morning or Evening Prayer from the Book of Common Prayer or one of the other easily available resources, or simply read from the Bible. Give God space in your life. Ten to fifteen minutes is an absolute minimum. And don't just talk at God; try listening too.

2. **Worship with others.** Don't just go when you feel like it or when you are fed. Go as an act of discipline. Worship weekly at a minimum. Begin the first hours of the first day of the week by devoting yourself to God.

3. **Find a small group.** Find a group of people with whom you can be truly honest and who can pray with you. Jesus and Mary Magdalene traveled with a group. Find your group. The group must meet at least weekly in order to truly become the kind of community that each of us needs to stay faithful. And you must be honest with one another. You must risk being vulnerable and telling the truth.[4]

If the mind is an organic thing, with tides and moving parts, then we must constantly pursue health and wellness. Mary did this by vigilant devotion to Jesus during his lifetime. She stayed close to him. And so should we.

---

4. A wonderful resource for discipleship groups can be found at *www.restorationproject.net*.

Thinking of Demons

Remember the movie *The Exorcist*? I will never forget Linda Blair's head spinning all the way around and her vomiting on the priest. That movie has come to represent demonic possession for many Americans today. We think of violent crazy behavior, horror movies, and evil acts. But what about the rest of us? Just because we don't act in strange and violent ways does not mean that we don't have to battle the darkness too. The early church included exorcism as part of baptism. They believed that all humans had demons or unclean spirits of one kind or another.[5] Hippolytus, who wrote in the second century, gave these detailed instructions for baptism:

> Those who are to receive baptism shall fast on the Preparation of the Sabbath. On the Sabbath, those who are to receive baptism shall all gather together in one place chosen according to the will of the bishop. They shall be commanded to pray and kneel. Then, laying his hand on them, he will exorcise every foreign spirit, so that they flee from them and never return to them. When he has finished exorcising them, he shall breathe on their faces and seal their foreheads, ears and noses. Then he shall raise them up.[6]

Thus by the year 215, church scholars had come to believe that every person was a breeding ground of unclean spirits and

---

5. Walter Wink, *Unmasking the Powers: The Invisible Forces that Determine Human Existence* (Philadelphia: Fortress Press Books, 1986), 53.

6. Hippolytus of Rome, *The Apostolic Tradition of Hippolytus of Rome* (Rome, 215 CE), ch. 20, verses 7–8.

must be exorcised before their baptism, even if they showed no signs of errant behavior or sinfulness. The presence of unclean spirits was considered part and parcel of the human condition prior to baptism. And even after baptism, it was common to seek the help of a priest when battling destructive thoughts or temptations. That was and still is the power and mystery of the sacrament of confession.

We may be able to control our behavior, but the truth is that all of us have unclean demonic thoughts. How many of us have looked in the mirror and told ourselves that we are ugly? How many of us have spoken to ourselves with hatred, telling ourselves that we are stupid or a failure? How many of us can become incapacitated by fear, believing that life is falling apart when we are struggling? How many struggle with internal dialogues of self-hatred? How many have thoughts of violence and anger toward others, turning that self-hatred outward? Hateful thoughts and feelings can startle us. They can repeat themselves like echoes. These inner voices are a kind of temptation. They come to all of us. They speak into our minds and must be identified and brought into the light.

Our deepest demonic thoughts are created when we absorb a hateful message as a child. These thoughts can sound like self-hatred, profound fear or anxiety, or simple black despair. Take for example the temptation to drink alcohol obsessively. Many of us have been tempted to get drunk, particularly if we grew up with parents who were alcoholics. But the demon voice can become a kind of possession when it takes over the mind, when it moves from an influence to a perceived reality. It happens when the person begins to believe that it is acceptable to drink herself into oblivion. Then the demon voice really takes on power.

All of us constantly battle negative, destructive, hateful, or fearful thoughts, thoughts of shame or guilt. The question is, do we realize that our minds are a battlefield? You see, demons and demonic voices do not want you to recognize them. They want to stay hidden. They want you to think that they are a part of you. They don't want to be examined or questioned. But God calls them all into the light.

Richard Rohr writes, "I understand 'possession by devils' as a primitive but absolutely truthful way of referring to what we now call addiction. In each case, the person is in some sense trapped by a larger force, and is powerless to do anything about it. The only cure for possession is 'repossession.' You have to be repossessed by Something Greater than the disease."[7] Jesus takes the thoughts of the human mind very seriously. They cannot be seen but they are an important part of the spiritual life. Even the one who looks with lust upon the spouse of another commits adultery in his mind, Jesus said. God help us all, for we all have dark thoughts and feelings. We all contend with the voices of demons that strive to tempt us away from God.

A Story

I knew Kathy years ago, when I was a young priest. She was very tall. She wore black clothes, combat boots, and carried a knife.

7. Richard Rohr, "Twelve Step Spirituality: Week One. In Need of Healing," adapted from *Breathing Under Water: Spirituality and the Twelve Steps* (Cincinnati: Franciscan Media, 2011), xii, xv, back cover.

She talked about wanting to pierce her tongue. She looked like the kind of person you didn't want to cross. She came not just on Sundays but began to drop by my office during the week. We would sit together in my office. She would perch on my sofa and wring her hands, unable to speak. She showed me where she had cut herself.

Over the months, Kathy told me what had happened to her mainly by writing it down on small scraps of paper that she would bring in with her. I encouraged her to see a therapist, but she still wanted to come by and talk to me. And this was her story.

Kathy was raped repeatedly, beginning around the age of four. Her uncle came to live with the family and he would find many ways to hurt her. Her mother was working full time and Kathy was often alone with her uncle. She didn't know how to explain what was happening, how to put it into words. She thought it was her fault. So she began washing her hands. Over and over again, many times a day, she would wash her hands until they became chapped and dry and red, and still she would continue to wash them. Her mother didn't understand why. It took her mother four years to discover what was really happening. Four years before it stopped.

There are many different kinds of vocabularies that we use when describing mental illness. Kathy suffered trauma as a child that resulted in mental health issues. The "voices" she internalized told her she was dirty and unworthy and that she should die. These voices and feelings originally came from outside her. They were instilled in her by trauma. They were a normal response to a horrible situation. Kathy was just trying to make sense of a crazy world. She was just trying to survive. She adopted demonic thoughts in her mind as a coping mechanism, to make sense of the horror of her childhood. She was overwhelmed with the voices of demons. These voices told her to hate herself, that she was unclean. These voices made her feel so bad that she wanted to die.

Kathy grew into this tough young woman who carried a knife in her pocket, took martial arts, and was plagued with anger and misery. We would pray together and she worked hard in therapy. When I moved away, I was certain she would be all right. But after many years, I heard from her mother that she had moved into an apartment all alone in a new city. She wanted to get away and see if she could make it on her own. She hung herself in her apartment.

Kathy is gone. I think of her every day and I write this book in the hopes that we may come to understand the forces that tormented her and how we can help others who suffer like her. I wonder if Mary Magdalene was hurt in a similar way.

6

Tempted

And Jesus, full of the Holy Spirit, returned from the Jordan and was led by the Spirit in the wilderness for forty days, being tempted by the devil.

—Luke 4:1

A more accurate translation for the Lord's Prayer is this: *And do not bring us to the time of trial, but rescue us from the evil one.* Jesus taught all of us to pray that we might be delivered from the evil one. All of us struggle with darkness.

Jesus did not have demons. He was simply too good for the normal kinds of demons that confront the rest of humanity. Demons couldn't tolerate Jesus's presence, so Jesus was tempted by the devil himself. And the devil could not enter Jesus's mind. He had to appear to Jesus as a separate being while Jesus was alone in the desert.

In the time of Jesus, temptation was considered to be a part of the human condition. The difference between Jesus and the rest of us is that Jesus was able to immediately identify temptation and say no to it. Jesus did this at the beginning of his ministry, before he did anything else. He was baptized in the Jordan River and then he went off alone, into the desert, to listen to the voice of God and to reject the devil. But Luke's gospel includes this tiny phrase that is so important. After Jesus defeats the devil and temptation, Luke writes: "[H]e [the devil] departed from him until an opportune time" (Luke 4:13). Even the Son of God had to contend with temptation, and that temptation was always waiting to return. I believe that Jesus had to reject temptation before he could help Mary Magdalene or anyone else. First, he had to master his own mind. And we too must identify our own temptations before we can serve God in any real way.

The Mystery of Temptation

All of us must contend with the fact that we will be tempted. Jesus gave us the gift of this awareness by facing this temptation himself. But Jesus was never possessed by demons. So what, then, is the relationship between demons and simple temptation?

The New Testament is not explicit as to how exactly temptation relates to unclean spirits or demons. Jesus was tempted in the desert by the devil himself. The devil used some basic temptations such as the temptation to eat when Jesus had vowed to fast. Of course, eating itself is a good thing. It is good to nourish the body. But almost any human behavior can become destructive if taken to an extreme. If one is unable to say no to any kind of food, one can die of overeating. There is true obesity in this country today. People are becoming so overweight as to endanger their health and well-being. Certainly, the act of eating has become for them a kind of temptation. It has been distorted to excess and can even kill a person. Thus temptation can begin in the simplest and smallest of ways by simply distorting a natural impulse or act. If left unchecked, temptation can expand from a minor distraction into impulses capable of destroying a person's life. Temptation is fed and grows when a person acquiesces to it. When refused, it loses all its power. It is the response of the person to the temptation that is so important.

Temptation can take on power if it is not cut off or restrained, as Jesus does in the desert. If we do not refuse temptation, if we engage it, converse with it, wrestle with, or God forbid, nurture it, it can easily take on a life of its own. When temptation takes up residence inside a person, when it is fed and nurtured, when it becomes a system of belief or a method of coping, it can become a demon. At what point does temptation become demonic influence? That is entirely individual to the person who is tempted.

All of us have learned behaviors or troubling memories that we cannot shake, thoughts that rise up to stifle our growth and creativity. So how can we identify our own demonic thoughts when they occur? How can we understand how our inner wounds and hurts can become the destructive voices that lurk inside our own minds? If we harness our wounds to justify our behavior, then we can allow a temptation to thrive within us. For example, if my dad drank alcohol all evening, perhaps I use that as an excuse to drink myself. I tell myself that it runs in the family, that it is genetic. Or I remember how he hit me and I use that pain to justify my own bad behavior, as if I am damaged goods and I can never be wholly well or kind. Wounds and suffering can be agents of great healing or they can become excuses to embrace temptation. The choice is up to us.

How can we prevent these disturbing thoughts, urges, and feelings from crippling our minds and preventing us from becoming who God is calling us to be?

I spoke earlier of the temptation of alcohol. Alcoholism is a demonic voice that speaks within the mind of a human being, justifying their behavior when that person is literally poisoning their body. It is the temptation of "let's have just one more drink" carried too far.

I met a man who was drinking himself to death. The temptation in his mind was powerful, performing great mental gymnastics to justify his drinking while creating excuses for the myriad of physical problems that he was encountering as his liver shut down. This man would rather die than confront his alcoholism. If that is not a great example of a temptation turned demonic, I don't know what is.

The Alcoholics Anonymous program was born in part in the Episcopal Church. Though its early specifically Christian language has been lost, it still speaks of a spiritual dimension and a higher power. The alcoholic is taught to rely on this higher power and to speak the stark truth about her addiction. This is the way the demons are fought, by prayer, reliance on God and community, reconciliation, and telling the truth. AA has all the elements to equip a person to battle the demons of alcoholism.

But even if you do not struggle with alcoholism, there are many other temptations that will enter your mind. Mental health is not some black line that we can draw in the sand

and step over to achieve success. All of us contend with dark thoughts and temptations. All of us must come to know the landscape of our own minds and how to identify thoughts that are wholesome from thoughts that are destructive. Every human being that I have come to know intimately has some place where unclean thoughts, demonic voices, and temptations find a home. Every one of us is in the midst of a spiritual battle between light and darkness, between Christ and the powers of evil. We have only to listen to our own thoughts to experience the reality of this battle. Once we can identify the voices of darkness, we can refuse to obey them. We can choose to be well, even if they continue to speak. Look at the life of the famous economist John Nash. He was a schizophrenic and did not want to take medication because it dulled his intellect. So he became accustomed to living with his illness. He saw people who were not there. He heard voices. But he simply identified them and then let them be. And in this way, he was able to do the work of a Nobel Prize winner and to witness to the light. He won the battle not by silencing the voices but simply by identifying them.

All of us face temptation. So how do we distinguish between the thoughts that are well and those that come from the darkness?

Coming to Know the Battlefield

Over the years, I have developed some clues for how to identify demonic thoughts. They are nothing more than a stab in the dark, but they have been helpful to me. These clues help me to understand my own thoughts, to know the difference between thoughts that are of God, thoughts that are just me, thoughts that are factual, and thoughts that are temptation and can lead to nothing but misery. Using these clues and their antidotes can lead to a healthier mind. *Health is not the absence of temptation, but merely the ability to see temptation for what it is.* It is the ability to let your destructive thoughts be and therefore to leave them powerless, devoid of your attention or focus.

Remember that the forces of darkness do not want to be brought into the light. That is why therapy and all good mental health efforts use truth as a weapon against illness. To tell the truth about what hurt you, to speak the words that come into your mind and cripple you—this is the beginning of the journey to health. When Jesus heals, he always casts the demons OUT. He brings them out of hiding and into the light. This is true of demonic thoughts as well. The greatest victory can come when the thoughts are brought out from hiding and into the light of the written or spoken word.

I have developed these clues after traveling the country, speaking and teaching numerous women and men, listening to how temptation works in their minds. I offer them as a road map. It is up to each individual to identify their own demonic thoughts and bring them into the light. You can do this by speaking them aloud or, better still, by writing them down. Do not elaborate on them, do not make excuses for them, do not filter them or try to make them sound more reasonable. Use the words that come into your mind without filters or interpretations and then look at them for what they are. See if they fall into any of these categories.

1. **The demonic always focuses on the self.** Temptation wants you consumed with yourself, either by feeling like a failure or like a great success. If you are thinking about your success or your failure, whether or not people like you, how you look . . . these thoughts may become temptation. Any kind of obsession with the self can lead to a demonic thought. When Jesus is tempted in the desert, all of the temptations have to do with the self. He is tempted to feed himself when he vowed to fast. He is tempted to throw himself off a cliff in order to test God. And he is tempted to take power for himself. It all has to do with ME. Never does the devil suggest that Jesus think of anyone else but himself.

   Remember that the concept of success is not of God, it is of this world. Success or failure are subjective, dangerous, and ever-moving targets, and they can rapidly become obsessions. If you are thinking about yourself all the time, look out for temptation.

   How do we counteract this obsession with the self? Pray for others. Give to others. Go visit someone. Remember that the Great Commandment is this: *Love God with all your heart, mind, and strength and love your neighbor as yourself.* According to this wisdom, the self is loved but it comes after the love of God and neighbor. Don't put yourself first or you will drown in self-absorption.

   What is so difficult about this temptation is that our culture encourages us in this self-absorption daily. We are told to buy, consume, eat, and pamper ourselves. While none of these things are bad in themselves, in our American culture the answer to all of our problems is focusing on the self. Even exercise can become idolatrous if done obsessively and only for the benefit of the self. American culture lies to us, suggesting that we can make ourselves happy by purchasing things, going on vacation, or eating the right foods. But we cannot make ourselves happy. Only God can do that. We cannot get caught in the illusion that our happiness is our primary purpose in life. Ironically, nothing seems to make us more miserable.

2. **Demonic thoughts are not original.** Temptation usually sounds like a broken record. Unlike God, whose revelation is always new and creative, the darkness will say the same things over and over and over again. Remember, the devil is not a creator. So if you are having the same thought over and over and over again, it might be temptation. In fact, you could probably rattle off some phrases that come up from time to time in your mind . . . voices that say that you are a loser or too fat or stupid . . . voices that tell you that no matter what you do, it is not enough. Demonic thoughts thrive on stealing your joy, so they are going to keep bombarding you with negativity, but it will most often be repetitive. There is nothing new that comes from the darkness.

This kind of repetition is easy to identify. Write these thoughts down and then just notice when they play over and over again in your mind. Their power is removed in the acknowledgement that they are nothing more than repetitive thoughts. Listen to them, get to know them, write them down, and bring them into the light, where they often sound ridiculous. If you are scared to tell your loved one what you are thinking because it sounds so stupid, it may be a demonic thought.

3. **The tempter tends to think that everything is a crisis.** Whatever is happening in your life is not just bad, it is awful. Patience, taking time—these are not qualities that the devil wants. The devil wants you to rush, to panic, to think that everything will not be all right. Demons do not want you to spend time alone with God, and when you sit down to do so, will often attack with temptation. The devil does not want you to think about the meaning of your life or whether you are treating your loved ones well. The devil wants you so busy that you do not recognize that you haven't had a meaningful conversation with your spouse in a week, or that your job is consuming your life, or that you have become desperately unhappy. The devil wants you too busy to notice.

Did you know that a frog, when placed in a pot of water, will stay in the water and allow its body to be boiled to death if you simply increase the temperature gradually? The frog never knows that his reality, the substance in which he sits, is becoming toxic, so he does not take himself out.

If you never spend time alone, how will you know when your busy life has become toxic or when the tipping point has occurred and you no longer know yourself? If you fill your days with noise, how will you listen?

The antidote to this kind of temptation is practicing silence. Start gently if your mind is accustomed to business and activity. Try listening to God while you walk. Open

your Bible. Carve out time for God. It is the most important thing that you can do in this life.

4. **Final clue.** Evil does not love. If you are having a thought
that is hyper-critical of yourself or others, a thought that
has no connection to love itself, unless it is purely factual or
informational, it is probably from the tempter. God would
have you love yourself and serve others. Ask yourself, is this
thought loving? If not, be aware and awake.

We all have demonic thoughts. We all have inner critics.
We all have a bit of instability come to us during our childhood, when the spirit is open and forming understanding. If
we are hurt or abused in any way, great darkness can enter our
minds and make a home. Even those who grew up in the most
stable and loving homes had moments of pain, hurt, and dis-
appointment. We live in a fallen world and all human beings
face temptation. The question is if you will have the courage
to bring your demonic thoughts into the light and see them for
what they are.

Mary Magdalene knew she was ill. In order for her to be
healed, she was willing to let herself be known by Jesus. She
came to him, to the brightness of his presence. She was willing
to admit that she needed help. And so do all of us.

7

The Providers

The twelve were with him, as well as some women who had been cured of evil spirits and infirmities: Mary, called Magdalene, from whom seven demons had gone out, and Joanna, the wife of Herod's steward Chuza, and Susanna, and many others, who provided for them out of their resources.

—LUKE 8:1–3

Magdala was a prosperous town on the shore of the Sea of Galilee. The word means "tower." A recent archaeological dig uncovered a synagogue at Magdala. The residents of Magdala were faithful and industrious.

Smithsonian magazine records the discovery of the synagogue with these words: "They'd found a synagogue from the time of Jesus, in the hometown of Mary Magdalene. Though big enough for just 200 people, it was, for its time and place, opulent. It had a mosaic floor; frescoes in pleasing geometries of red, yellow and blue; separate chambers for public Torah readings, private study and storage of the scrolls, a bowl outside for the ritual washing of hands."[1]

---

1. Ariel Sabar, "The Search for Jesus: New Archaeology from Galilee to Jerusalem," *Smithsonian* 46 (2016): 45.

In the center of the sanctuary, archaeologists discovered a stone. Intricate carvings of a variety of symbols adorn all sides of the stone, among them menorahs and a chariot of fire. This stone of Magdala may in fact be one of the greatest archaeological discoveries in decades. Analyzing the stone could lead to new insights into the world of Galilee in the time of Jesus and the life of the village where Mary Magdalene lived.

As Magdala was a prosperous town, perhaps Mary was born into a wealthy family. What happened to her when her demons became evident? Would her family have had the capacity to care for her? Would they have hidden her away or were her demons too violent to be kept secret? We may never have answers to these questions.

What we know is that Luke lists Mary Magdalene first among a group of women and men *who provided for them out of their resources.* Remember again, the simple passage from Luke:

> Soon afterward he went on through cities and villages, proclaiming and bringing the good news of the kingdom of God. And the twelve were with him, as well as some women who had been cured of evil spirits and infirmities: Mary, called Magdalene, from whom seven demons had gone out, and Joanna, the wife of Herod's steward Chuza, and Susanna, and many others, who provided for them out of their resources.

> —LUKE 8:1–3

Did Mary have resources of her own? It is possible that it was the other women who had resources; the passage is not clear. Luke does not specify who owned what. Whether she gave her money or just her toil and sweat does not seem to be important. The important thing is that, in some way, Mary was among those who provided for Jesus.

Seldom do we consider who fed Jesus. He walked everywhere with his disciples. Crowds were gathering around him, exhausting him with their needs and desires. Jesus was healing, teaching, walking, casting out demons. Behind the scenes, someone had to be thinking about where they were going to sleep that night. Someone had to buy bread, cook fish, find something to drink. These basic physical needs were provided for by women and perhaps by the disciples as well, and by hosts who took Jesus and his followers in along the way. Some of those who provided for Jesus are named and some are not. We do know that women were expected to cook, clean, and generally look after men. It was their usual role in society. All women were trained to cook from an early age. It was a necessary means for survival. The ideal woman was a provider in the Hebrew scriptures. Proverbs puts it this way:

> She gets up while it is still night and provides food for her household and tasks for her servant-girls . . . She looks well to the sons of her household, and does not eat the bread of idleness.
>
> —PROVERBS 31:15, 27

For these reasons, I believe that the women who accompanied Jesus would have also served him physically by cooking, cleaning, and doing other manual tasks as the group traveled. I think it is time for the women who accompanied Jesus to have a name like that of the disciples. I want to call them *the providers.*

Everywhere that Jesus walked and taught, the providers must have been working. Remember that this was not an era of fast food or grocery stores. Fish had to be bought fresh from the fishermen themselves. Preparing meals was no small feat in a world with no refrigeration, especially when you had no idea where you would be sleeping the next night. Fires had to be made outside. Food and water had to be packed each day, for they often walked for miles. Jesus traveled with twelve men! That's a lot of food, a lot of water, a lot of washing. These women were concerned not only with where Jesus would sleep and eat, but even about repairing his sandals, washing his clothing, and bandaging his wounds. They would have heard much of what Jesus taught and seen his miracles, but that was not their primary focus. Their first priority was to serve Jesus, to keep him fed and safe.

The disciples were counted; the providers were not. The disciples were listed by name; only a few of the providers' names are recorded. I think it is important to give these women credit, however, for they did have an essential role. They were the tech crew, the behind-the-scenes laborers, the producers, the hard-working silent support. They were important.

Jesus often spoke with harsh words about the wealthy. He said that it was harder for a camel to go through the eye of a needle than for a rich man to enter heaven. But here were women of some means who gave of what they had to make sure that Jesus was cared for. Magdalene and the others provide a role model for those of us who have resources. We can be providers too.

Throughout history, so many women have been quiet providers. Without the mothers and wives of the great men that led the world, where would we be? Every single one of us was born from some woman who nurtured us within her body for nine months so that we might live. And hidden within the pages of the gospels, there is so much activity and effort that has never been acknowledged: women who quietly went about cooking, cleaning, washing, and drying so that Jesus and the disciples could spread the news of the kingdom. Let us not forget their work. It was just as important as that of the men.

Humanity is so interconnected. We would not be here were it not for the care and concern of one or more parents. Someone fed us, someone washed us, someone may still be providing for us in some way. Mary the mother of Jesus cared for him when he was a child; she kept him safe and protected him along with Joseph. When Jesus became a man, Mary Magdalene and the other women cared for him. Even Jesus needed someone to lean on so that he could do the work of God. None of us is called to total solitude. Even the hermit must have someone bring him food. God created us to live in relationship with one another and to provide for each other.

When battling demons, it is very helpful to serve another human being. How many of us can manage to be miserable when we are serving food to another person? How many of us can wallow in self-pity while acting generously? Mary's recipe for health was not only to stay close to her Lord but to serve him with all her means.

Matthew Lieberman is a neuroscientist. In his recent book *Social*, Lieberman argues that human beings are healthier in community. Connecting with others is a fundamental human need, like water or food. When a human being is isolated or cut off from others, when relationships break down or dissolve, we are hurt. The great American myth of individual success and happiness is just that, a myth. It's really not about me. It's about us.

The human being is designed to live in community, and I believe mental health is nurtured best in community. We were not designed to live alone. God made us in pairs. Jesus sent out the disciples in pairs. We are not capable of seeing ourselves clearly, our faults, our aspirations, our behaviors. We need one another to achieve mental balance and health. We need honest feedback, nurture, and love. We are social creatures, and Mary Magdalene knew that to maintain her health, she must learn to live in community.

In her book *Happiness*, Joan Chittister writes that relatedness, or the process in which we live and work in community, is essential for any kind of human thriving. She writes, "To be a 'social creature' means that, as a species, we really don't do anything alone. We can't do anything alone. What the awareness of that insight implies for happiness, as well as for any other dimension of life, takes the whole concept of 'individualism,' shakes it by the back of the neck and turns upside down everything we have ever taken for granted about our own invincibility, our jealously guarded 'independence,' our barely disguised sense of lordliness."[2] To be human means that we need one another. We were simply not designed to live in total isolation. We were designed to live in relationship. Mary Magdalene stayed well by

---

2. Joan Chittister, *Happiness* (Grand Rapids, MI: Wm. B. Eerdmans Publishing, 2011), 106.

living in and among the disciples and Jesus. She relied on life in community to keep her mental and spiritual balance. This was an essential aspect of her health.

When Mary Magdalene suffered from demons, she probably suffered alone. She alone was possessed. When she was healed by Jesus, she became part of a community. She stayed with him and with the disciples. Part of her cure was a life lived in the company of others, providing for them, caring for them, and probably learning from them. The life of the provider is a wonderful path for those who want to find health and stability.

Mary Magdalene would stay with Jesus even when the other disciples ran away. She would stay with Jesus even as he suffered and died on the cross.

8

∽

Being There

When I think of the cross, I tend to picture Jesus alone. After all, he does cry out, "My God, my God, why have you forsaken me?" (Matthew 27:46). Not only was his death immensely painful, but it was also incredibly lonely. He felt that God had abandoned him. The disciples ran away while his enemies laughed at him and turned their backs to throw dice for his clothing. Scripture leaves us with the ominous feeling that Jesus was left alone to die.

However, if you read the gospels carefully, it becomes clear that Jesus was not alone when he was crucified, nor was he only surrounded by his enemies. It is true that the disciples fled, but there were women who remained. In all four of the gospel accounts there are women who do not leave. And the first among the women is Mary Magdalene.

Matthew, Mark, Luke, and John all describe the crucifixion in different ways. Matthew felt that it was important to mention that Jesus hung on the cross for about three hours. Luke describes how Jesus talked to criminals who were crucified on either side of him. John tells us that Jesus instructed his beloved disciple to take care of his mother. Each of the gospels records different women as being present. But in all the gospel accounts, Mary Magdalene is there.

Matthew

> Many women were also there, looking on from a distance; they had followed Jesus from Galilee and had provided for him. Among them were Mary Magdalene, and Mary the mother of James and Joseph, and the mother of the sons of Zebedee.
>
> —MATTHEW 27:55–56

Matthew does not mention the presence of the women at the cross until after Jesus has breathed his last breath and the centurion has proclaimed, "Truly this man was God's Son!" (Matthew 27:54). It is as if the presence of the women was an afterthought, not worth mentioning during the passion itself but something that Matthew added on to flesh out the scene after Jesus had died. The women were part of the backdrop, part of the scenery. Matthew was nearly done writing his account of the crucifixion when he thought to himself, "Oh, and I forgot to mention that the women were there!" How invisible women were in Jesus's day! But their invisibility actually served them on that day, because they were not noticed or taken seriously. The soldiers simply overlooked their presence. They were not important enough to be punished. This gave the women a kind of freedom to remain with Jesus when he suffered. Their insignificance enabled them to stay close to their Lord.

Matthew writes that there were many women. We have no idea how many. He doesn't count. He mentions a few by name and Mary Magdalene is first on his list. Like Luke, Matthew takes the time to mention that these women provided for Jesus. Mary Magdalene is named along with Mary the mother of James and Joseph. The third woman mentioned was the mother of the sons of Zebedee, but Matthew does not tell us her name. So at least one woman was the mother of disciples. When her sons ran from the shame of Golgotha, their mother stayed put.

Matthew mentions that these women were looking on *from a distance*. This is a vague description but we can hope that if they could see Jesus, then he could see them. They stood within his sight as a source of strength and comfort, too far away to speak but still visible to the one they loved who was dying. I hope that Jesus looked at them and found strength.

Mark

> There were also women looking on from a distance; among them were Mary Magdalene, and Mary the mother of James the younger and of Joses, and Salome.
>
> —MARK 15:40

Mark's account is quite similar to Matthew's but for a few minor differences. Mark also lists the women only after Jesus has taken his last breath. Mark also mentions that there were many women and that they looked on from a distance. He mentions that these women provided for Jesus, but he also lists other women who may not have been providers but who had followed Jesus to Jerusalem. The three that Mark lists by name are: Mary

Magdalene, Mary the mother of James the younger and of Joses, and Salome. Mary the mother of James and Joses could certainly be the same person as the Mary mother of James and Joseph in Matthew. Could Salome be the name of the mother of the sons of Zebedee? We may never know. But one thing is for sure: Mary Magdalene is again listed first.

Luke

> But all his acquaintances, including the women who had followed him from Galilee, stood at a distance, watching these things.
>
> —LUKE 23:49

Luke's account is by far the most vague. He does not mention any of the women by name. But he does recall that there was a group of women who had accompanied Jesus in Galilee and, since he listed Mary Magdalene as one of them earlier in the gospel, it can be assumed that she was present as well.

John

> Meanwhile, standing near the cross of Jesus were his mother, and his mother's sister, Mary the wife of Clopas, and Mary Magdalene. When Jesus saw his mother and the disciple whom he loved standing beside her, he said to his mother, "Woman, here is your son." Then he said to the disciple, "Here is your mother." And from that hour the disciple took her into his own home.
>
> —JOHN 19:25–27

It was important for John to record the last will and testament of Jesus. As he is dying, he takes care to provide for Mary his mother, asking his beloved disciple to care for her as if she were his own mother. Tradition tells us that his wishes were honored and Mary moved in with John the beloved disciple immediately after Jesus's death. But even in the midst of Jesus giving these instructions in the gospel, Mary Magdalene is mentioned by name. She is not forgotten but stands quietly by as Jesus cares for his mother. Also present were Jesus's aunt and Mary the wife of Clopas.

In John's gospel, these women stand much closer to the cross. If Jesus had this conversation while hanging on the cross, he was speaking while his lungs were filling with fluid, as happens when a body is crucified. Jesus could not have spoken very loudly. The women would have had to have been close by to hear his words and to reply to him. John describes simply that they *were standing near the cross*. This is a much more intimate scene than in the other three gospels.

Being There

Mary Magdalene is not recorded as saying anything at the cross, but she is there. She is present and it is her presence that is immensely important. Mary Magdalene is the only consistently named presence at the cross in all of the gospel accounts. She does not rush off. She does not hide. She does not give advice. She does not pound on the cross or try to get him down. She just stands there in silence. She is present with Jesus as he takes his last breath.

When someone that we love is in pain, the hardest thing to do is to just be present. Our fear whispers that we need to try to fix the situation, make suggestions, or even pretend that our loved one is all right when they are not. I am terribly guilty of launching into advice when one of my loved ones is in pain, but sometimes the only way out is through the pain. Sometimes we just can't fix it. Sometimes the only thing that we can do is just not leave. Strangely, the best healing often comes when we just listen to our loved ones and let them be.

How did Mary Magdalene have the courage to stay? Why didn't she run and hide along with the men? It is not easy to stay present when someone is in excruciating pain. How did she have the strength? Was it the sheer power of Jesus's presence that drew her in and calmed her fear, or was it something more?

I wonder at times about these women who traveled together and served Jesus. Did they find comfort in each other? Did they find that together they could do much more than any one of them could have done alone?

Two years ago, I held hands with three women before a surgery early one morning in a hospital waiting room. There was an immediate presence among us as we prayed. I felt a mystical strength as we spoke and listened to one another. The experience was so profound that I asked the three of them if we could meet once a week for an hour and just pray together. To my delight and surprise, they all agreed.

We meet on the third floor of St. John's Cathedral in a small chapel. We talk about our lives and then simply join hands and speak to God. Sometimes we sing. Sometimes we sit in silence. Without fail, every time we gather, there is a presence so strong and so vibrant that it fills the room in which we sit. I find that my life has been mysteriously amplified. I am more courageous, more committed to my marriage, more attentive to my children, all because of the presence and prayers of these women. I find strength when we connect with God together.

Jesus said that when two or three are gathered together in his name, God is in the midst of them. I imagine that Mary Magdalene and these women, whoever they were and whatever their names, prayed together, and from that community of prayer came strength that none of them could have had alone. They found that they could be more together than they were apart.

I also wonder if Mary's battles with demons and her healing left her stronger than most. They say that scar tissue is stronger than ordinary skin. Did she emerge with a strength and courage beyond her years? Maybe her past experiences made her wiser and more able to be present with him even when things became unbearable for almost everyone else. Maybe her struggles made her strong enough to stand at the foot of the cross.

Could it be that God uses the most painful parts of our lives to make it possible for us to truly listen to others who struggle, to make us strong enough to be truly present?

The greatest gift that we can give to our loved ones is the gift of our undivided attention. Mary Magdalene stood there at the cross and she just was. She did nothing. She said nothing. She just stood there, not running away but just being with Jesus while he suffered the worst kind of agony imaginable.

9

Essential Rest

After the sabbath, as the first day of the week was dawning, Mary Magdalene and the other Mary went to see the tomb.

—Matthew 28:1

When the Sabbath was over, Mary Magdalene, and Mary the mother of James, and Salome, bought spices, so that they might go and anoint Him.

—Mark 16:1

But on the first day of the week, at early dawn, they came to the tomb, taking the spices that they had prepared.

—Luke 24:1

It is a wonder to me that Mary Magdalene observed the Sabbath after Jesus's crucifixion. She and the other women did not come to the grave on the Sabbath day. Despite their acute grief, despite the trauma that they had endured, despite the pain and shock and brutality of watching their master die, they waited. They continued to observe the rest required of all devout Jews.

When I consider the excuses that I come up with when trying to practice a life of prayer, this puts me to shame. I find reasons not to sit still with God that are so mundane. I think to myself, *I am tired. I am too busy. I need to get to my next appointment. I need to phone someone. I have laundry to do.* The list of excuses is endless. And all of them are nothing in comparison with the pain that Mary Magdalene had to endure.

The providers had accompanied Jesus for three years. They had taken care of his every physical need. And now his body lay bloodied and bruised in a tomb. The heat of Israel would have meant that in the space of a Sabbath day, Jesus's body would have started to decompose. They had to wait while heat and insects claimed his body. If ever there was an excuse for breaking the observance of the Sabbath, this would have been it. But something in Mary Magdalene and the other women told them to continue to practice the kind of prayer that they had practiced while Jesus was alive. Something told them that to rush and break the prayer practice by which he had lived would be to dishonor his memory. So they stayed put on the Sabbath, and I'm sure that the day must have seemed to last forever.

One of the great temptations of our age is the temptation to rush. The tempter would have us believe that everything is a crisis, that we cannot wait and take the time to sit with God. Life is too busy, too crazy. Our appointments are too important. We cannot take time to sit still in prayer when there is so much to do! Projects left undone are like open wounds to us, crying out for our immediate attention. A job left undone is a failure. We must finish everything *now*!

But no one had more to do than those women on that Sabbath day. No one had more on their minds, more pressure to get up and *do something*. And yet they did not succumb. They did not do anything. They just sat still with God. They rested.

If Mary and the other providers rested after a trauma this significant, if Mary Magdalene and the others could leave Jesus's body bloodied and decomposing, perhaps we can learn to leave our houses messy and our projects undone for just a little longer while we take the time to pray. After all, God's notion of time is different from our own. Problems do not need to be solved in an instant for the One who created the heavens and formed the mountains and the seas. If we want God to shape our lives, we must slow down and observe the moments when God invites us to pray.

10

Coming to the Tomb

> Mary Magdalene and the other Mary were there, sitting opposite the tomb.
>
> —MATTHEW 27:61

I have wondered if there is some kind of correlation between true genius and the capacity to face darkness. Consider Vincent van Gogh. He was depressed. He had a nervous breakdown when the woman he wanted to marry refused his advances. He couldn't hold a job. He ended up committing suicide. There were also times when he could move through his darkness to create paintings of genius. His paintings were so original that their impact on the artistic world was not felt during his lifetime. Only after his death did people begin to recognize his creative gift. Was there a correlation between the originality of his art and his battles with darkness? Did his journey through his pain enable him to find a kind of expression that was entirely new?

In one of his letters to his brother, Van Gogh wrote about seeing light in the midst of the darkness while sitting alone in the woods: "The ground was lighter and darker red-brown, all the more so because of the shadows of trees that threw bands across . . . (I)t was only while painting that I noticed how much light there still was in that darkness."[1]

I do not believe that depression makes one creative, nor do I accept the age-old belief that the artistic tend to be more depressed. Depression is not something to be sought after—it is an agonizing state that must never be idolized. But I do believe that one must have the capacity to look into the darkness in order to experience true inspiration. In other words, one cannot avoid feelings of despair and suffering if one wants to truly listen to God's work in the world. Van Gogh did not shy away from darkness. He looked at it deeply. He explored it. It was this kind of courage and honesty that contributed to his genius.

I believe that there is a reason why Mary Magdalene was the first to witness the resurrection. This reason is linked directly with her capacity to approach the darkness of the tomb. Mary Magdalene had faced profound darkness in her own life. Her past experiences gave her the capacity to not only tolerate the darkness but to search for Christ within it. Because of her courage and tenacity, Mary was there at the break of dawn to witness the resurrection.

Sometimes the only way to find the light is to face the darkness, to go and sit by the grave. Running from pain and despair does not save us. We run from pain instinctively, but true life exists when we stop running and approach the darkness looking for light on the other side.

---

1. From a letter dated September 3, 1882, in *Letters from Vincent van Gogh* (Washington, DC: The Trinity Forum, 2016), 7.

The Darkness

As a parish priest, I see the same phenomenon year after year. People do not want to go through the darker parts of the gospel story. Every year the church is packed for Palm Sunday when we celebrate Jesus's ride into Jerusalem on a donkey. The crowd thins drastically on Maundy Thursday as Jesus shares the Last Supper with his friends. That night, when Jesus begged his friends to stay awake with him, a faithful few vow to stay awake with Jesus all night. When Jesus hangs on the cross to die, a small fraction of the congregation comes to worship. Then, without fail, the church is packed again on Easter to celebrate the good stuff.

I have tried to explain that we cannot really know the gift of the resurrection without the experience of Jesus's cross and burial, but my words fall flat. We all instinctively want to avoid suffering. We want to leap from the celebration of Palm Sunday to the celebration of Easter. But how can we understand the joy of Easter without the struggle of the cross?

Many churches in America have made the mistake of catering to people's desires and promising prosperity through the gospel. It is true that coming to know Jesus can bring peace, but nowhere does the gospel claim that becoming a Christian will make your life easier, let alone make you rich. The gospel becomes just another self-help program if the cross is eliminated; it becomes another social club without a clear vision of Jesus's life and work among the poor and the outcast. Fully understanding the light requires that the darkness be involved in some way. As Barbara Brown Taylor puts it in her book

Learning to Walk in the Darkness, "They have a hard time warming up to any kind of salvation that divides reality in two and asks them to forsake the bottom half."[2]

There is no part of the night that is darker than the moment just before the sun rises. Mary Magdalene walked to the tomb in that period of the night, the darkest period. She was willing to search for even a remnant of Jesus in that darkness. Was she afraid? She had to have been. I cannot imagine otherwise. She was headed to a dead body in the darkest part of the night. But that was where love was leading her.

In our pursuit of comfort and ease, we often run from the darkness. But then someone we love becomes ill and we are forced to make a decision between what is easier and what is more loving. The path of love takes us into the dark, there is no doubt, but at least we have Mary Magdalene walking ahead of us.

Approaching the Darkness with Friends

> After the Sabbath, as the first day of the week was dawning,
> Mary Magdalene and the other Mary went to see the tomb.
>
> —MATTHEW 28:1

In the first three gospels, Mary does not go to the tomb alone. She goes with friends. Though the names are different in the various gospels, this fact is immensely important. Mary did not

---

2. Barbara Brown Taylor, *Learning to Walk in the Darkness* (New York: Harper One, 2014), 12.

do this alone. She found strength in her companions. Even in John's gospel, when Mary sees the empty tomb, the first thing that she does is to get Peter and John.

In fact, the majority of Mary Magdalene's relationship with Jesus would have been based within the context of community. They traveled in community, ate in community, slept in community. This notion that Mary Magdalene and Jesus were married or had some kind of affair is highly unlikely. The truth was that they were part of a small group of disciples and providers.

Mary did not go through the darkness alone. She wept and prayed and felt afraid all in the company of others who shared her grief. God does not want us to hide our darkness from others. Strength comes when we are willing to share our pain and journey alongside those we love. Our darkness can be seen more clearly by others than by ourselves. There is great relief and great courage that comes when we are willing to allow others to see the truth about our struggles and our pain.

11

Breaking Open

Early on the first day of the week, while it was still dark, Mary
Magdalene came to the tomb and saw that the stone had been
removed from the tomb. So she ran and went to Simon Peter
and the other disciple, the one whom Jesus loved, and said to
them, "They have taken the Lord out of the tomb, and we do
not know where they have laid him."

—JOHN 20:1–2

Peter and the beloved disciple trust Mary Magdalene enough
to believe her words and they run immediately to the tomb.
The beloved disciple reaches the tomb first but waits for Peter
before going in. They see that there is no body and they notice
that the linen has been placed to the side and that the face cloth
is folded up in a place by itself. Peter and the beloved disciple
then run off to tell the others.

But Mary Magdalene does not leave. She stays, crying, by
the tomb. Just as she had remained at the cross, she cannot seem
to leave the site where Jesus's body once laid. It is there that she
sees the Risen Christ.

Vulnerability

> The most transformative and resilient leaders that I have
> worked with over the course of my career have . . . the abil-
> ity and willingness to lean in to discomfort and vulnerability.
>
> —BRENÉ BROWN[1]

> But Mary stood weeping outside the tomb.
>
> —JOHN 20:11

People often apologize when they cry in church but nothing is
more beautiful to me. It means that a word, a feeling, a piece
of music really reached them. It means that they are willing,
at some level, to trust that church is safe. It means that they
are allowing themselves to feel. Tears are a gift. Telling the truth
about your pain is a gift. We don't come to know one another
deeply by sharing our successes; we come to know one another,
to truly connect, when we share our pain.

To be vulnerable is to allow yourself to be known. We all
struggle and yet we are afraid to admit our pain. It is easier just
to hide behind a façade of normalcy. But true intimacy comes
when we are willing to risk being known, flaws and all. True
intimacy arises when we admit that we struggle. It is no coin-
cidence that Mary Magdalene witnessed the Risen Christ right
when she was most vulnerable, right when she was broken open,
crying her eyes out.

In her book, *Time to Think*, Nancy Kline argues that allowing ourselves to cry and express our feelings openly actually

---

1. Brené Brown, *Rising Strong: The Reckoning, the Rumble, the Revolution* (New York: Spie-gle and Grau, 2015), 8.

increases clarity of thought: "Our society is terrified of tears, of anger, and of fear. We have mixed up the release of pain with the cause of pain . . . repression of feeling represses clear thinking. It muddles the mind."[2] Kline argues that crying actually makes you smarter. The expression of feelings makes space in the mind for innovation, creativity, and change. Crying opens our minds to new possibilities.

There was Mary, kneeling by an empty tomb, crying. And just at the moment when she broke apart, Jesus came. He came when she admitted that she had hit rock bottom, when she had no answers left, when she allowed herself to just feel. He came just when she expressed the depth of her pain, when she let it all come out. It took Mary Magdalene's breaking open for her to see resurrection. We too must be vulnerable if we are to witness God's grace.

Grace

When I was visiting a Methodist church about ten years ago, a man asked me a question at the end of a class I had taught: "What do you think of grace?" he said.

I'll never forget the earnest look on his face when he asked the question. I had no idea how to answer, because I did not know much about grace. Grace was a word that some Christians used, a blanket term that was generally positive. I had no idea. It took me another decade to discover what grace really was.

Grace comes only from God. It is a surprising and unexpected outpouring of love that is given to us freely. God forgives

---

2. Nancy Kline, *Time to Think: Listening to Ignite the Human Mind* (London: Octopus Publishing House, 1999), 75.

us and adores us despite our complete idiocy. The irony of grace is that it comes to us not when we earn it or deserve it, but often when we feel most lost, most broken, most vulnerable. The Savior comes to those who admit that they need a savior. So long as we are convinced that we can handle this life on our own, we cannot experience grace despite its outpouring from God.

Intimacy and Innovation

I believe that there is a direct link between intimacy with God and vulnerability. If we want to be close to Jesus, we must find a way to accept God's love when we are broken. The first step to accepting God's love at our most broken is simply looking at the messes we have made and being honest about our limitations. We must sit there, in the dust, near the grave that contains all the things that have died in our lives, crying. We invite God to enter when we admit that we can't do it ourselves, when we begin to understand that God loves us in spite of the fact that we are lost and broken. The best writer and researcher on vulnerability is Brené Brown. She writes about the importance of vulnerability: "Owning our story can be hard, but not nearly as difficult as spending our lives running from it. Embracing our vulnerabilities is risky, but not nearly as dangerous as giving up on love and belonging and joy—the experiences that make us the most vulnerable. Only when we are brave enough to explore the darkness will we discover the infinite power of our light."[3]

---

3. Brené Brown, quote found online at *https://www.goodreads.com/quotes/357565-owning-our-story-can-be-hard-but-not-nearly-as*.

When Mary Magdalene sat by that tomb weeping, she was in immense pain, but she was also broken open. In her pain, she had created a space, an opening for God to enter. She made room for the immense joy that can come only from God. She could have run from the pain and the grave but she did not. She stayed near an empty tomb, in the unexplainable fear of what she then thought was a crime scene. She stayed and she cried out to God. And God came to her.

Brené Brown goes on to write, "Vulnerability is the birthplace of innovation, creativity, and change."[4] There is a mysterious space created when a person is broken open and does not hide. God is able to enter that space in a new way, with new life, with resurrected life. When Adam and Eve disobeyed God, they realized that they were naked and they hid in shame and fear. When we acknowledge that we are naked but we do not run or flee from shame, we invite God to return to us as God. We return to the Eden where miracles can take place.

Mary Magdalene was a wreck that day. She was vulnerable and broken, but she did not hide. And God came to her in a newness of life that would change the world. When we have the courage to be vulnerable, we too have the opportunity to see resurrection.

Why is it that we change more from our suffering than from our success? We learn from pain because it breaks us open to see more clearly, to ask for help, to admit that we don't have all the answers, that we cannot do this alone.

---

4 Brené Brown, *Daring Greatly: How the Courage to be Vulnerable Transforms the Way We Live, Love, Parent, and Lead* (New York: Avery Publishing, 2012).

Humility

The root word for humility is the same as the word for human, *humus*. I believe that one of the reasons Mary Magdalene was the first one to witness the resurrection had to do with her ability to let herself be human. That sounds strange, doesn't it? Of course we all know we are human! But the truth is that many of us still live under the delusion that we may be more like God.

We live with the delusion of total control. We really believe that we can make ourselves happy if we just orchestrate the perfect set of circumstances: ideal job, ideal spouse, kids or no kids, income, vacations, etc. We think that tragedy and illness are unfortunate accidents that happen to some people but probably won't happen to us, and if they do, we ask why God is punishing us. We believe, essentially, that we can build Eden if we just work hard enough.

Mary sat in the dust crying. She did not try to fix the mess. She did not run away like the disciples when she saw the empty tomb. She sat. She stayed with the situation that was in front of her. She was humble. A human feeling—that's all. She let herself be and that is when God came. God came in a way that she never could have planned or expected. God was able to be God because Mary was able to be human. And what happened next defies all rational explanation.

12

⁓

Encountering Angels

As she wept, she bent over to look into the tomb; and she saw two angels in white, sitting where the body of Jesus had been lying, one at the head and the other at the feet. They said to her, "Woman, why are you weeping?" She said to them, "They have taken away my Lord, and I do not know where they have laid him."

—JOHN 20:11–13

Mary Magdalene began her life with demons and ended her story with angels. She was able to progress from horror to enlightenment, from darkness to light, from evil to good, from lies to the truth. She models for us the direction that we all wish to move—from suffering to the bounteous joy that can only come from God. We all want to grow towards the light.

Angels appear in the gospels to initiate a kind of radical in-breaking of God's presence into human lives. They appear to announce Jesus's birth to Joseph and Mary in Matthew's and Luke's gospels. And they appear to announce the second rebirth, the resurrection of Jesus. They serve as a kind of wake-up call. *Look!* God says. *Pay attention. Something really new is going on here. I am sending a special messenger to awaken you to this new reality.* Angels appear to wait on God and Jesus both in heaven and at particular moments in Jesus's life, namely after his temptations in the desert and in the Garden of Gethsemane. But angels appear to the rest of us to give us a message that perhaps we could not receive any other way. They come as the bearers of radical inspiration, messengers of life-altering news.

The word *angel* is another of those broad umbrella terms used in the ancient Greek and Hebrew of the Bible. It means so much more than any one English word can define. In the Greek, it can mean simply messenger, one who relays an important message, one who is sent. This messenger could be either human or celestial, the word does not specify. Only context can determine the type of messenger and sometimes that is left up to mystery. In Matthew and John, the word ἄγγελος ("angel") is used for the ones who meet Mary Magdalene at the tomb. In Mark, she is met by a young man and in Luke by two men, both dressed in something so bright it catches their attention. Luke and Mark never tell us if these men would be considered angels, just that they were there and that they wore white. Perhaps Luke and Mark were not certain who they were. In all accounts, these angels or men come before Jesus. They announce his arrival, just as they did when he was born.

Angelic Arrivals

Angels and demons are both mysterious. Both are mentioned over and over again in scripture, but many Christians do not believe in them today. Of course, we all know that the angels are the good guys, the representatives of God, whereas demons are servants of the devil, the fallen angel, Satan. But there are many other qualities that distinguish angels from demons. One crucial difference between angels and demons is the simple fact that angels do not possess a person. Rather, angels seem to do the opposite. Angels always appear outside a person, either in reality or in a dream. And they only appear to a select few.

As agents of God's love, angels do not invade or intrude upon a person's mind. They offer messages from outside the mind, waiting for a person who is open to seeing them and to listening to their message. They seem to have the highest respect for the person to whom they appear, often reassuring that person not to be afraid.

In Matthew, the angel appears with an earthquake that no one can miss; even the guards witness the appearance of the angel as he sits on the stone that he has rolled back from the tomb. The angel's appearance is like lightening and the guards are terrified. The angel addresses only the women with the familiar words: *Do not be afraid!*

In Mark, Mary Magdalene, Mary the mother of James, and Salome approach the tomb where they encounter a young man dressed in a white robe. He also tells them not to be afraid and instructs them to tell the others that Jesus has risen.

In Luke, Mary Magdalene and Joanna, Mary the mother of James, and some other women look into the empty tomb, first seeing nothing. Then suddenly, there stand two men in dazzling clothes. These men tell the women that Jesus has risen.

And finally, in John, only Mary Magdalene is able to see the two angels that sit at the head and the feet of where Jesus's body would have lain. The disciples look into the tomb and see nothing but an empty tomb with a linen cloth folded up and lying by the side. But Mary sees angels, and they serve as the transition to her witness of the Risen Christ himself.

We will never know why angels appeared to certain people and not others. Why did Mary Magdalene see the angels sitting where Jesus's body would have lain but the disciples did not see them? Was it the intensity of her search for Jesus that enabled her to see them? Were the disciples rushing and not really looking? I have always believed that to witness an angel, one must be awake—that it is the state of one's awareness that determines their ability to receive a messenger from God.

Agents of Transition

When I want to give my husband big news, I will often prepare him first. He does not like surprises, so I find that it's best to ask him to sit down and give me his undivided attention before launching into whatever life-changing event that I want to report. Angels serve as agents of transition or transformation. They stand at the intersection of two kinds of reality and invite their observers to consider a new kind of world, a world in which resurrection is possible.

Can we see angels today? Since the scriptures are not clear about who can in fact be angels, it is very possible. Angels can be people living right alongside you in this world. Angels can be regular human beings. Anyone who gives you news that is so radically good as to change your life could be considered an angel.

There is a scene in the movie *Walk the Line*, when Johnny Cash almost dies from detoxing after being addicted to drugs. The woman who would later become his wife, June Carter, and her parents stay by his side as he sweats, hallucinates, and passes in and out of consciousness. When he finally emerges from his drugged state, June is sitting on his bed with a bowl of fresh raspberries for him. As he tastes them, Johnny Cash looks at June and says, "You've been here all this time? You're an angel."

"I had a friend," June says. "You are my friend."

Johnny begins to open up to her about the demonic voices that have driven him into his addiction. "I am nothing," Cash says, echoing the words that his father spoke to him after his older brother's death, words that have plagued his mind his whole life, making him want to die.

June looks at him and begins to cry. "You are not nothing," she says.

"But I have made so many mistakes," he responds.

"You have made a few," she replies, "but you are not nothing. You are a good man. And this is your chance to make things right. This is your chance. This is your chance."

In that moment, June Carter is an angel. She becomes one by bearing a message of such incredible hope and acceptance that Johnny Cash hears her. She does not negate his mistakes nor deny that he has hurt people. But at the same time, she gives him a message of hope. Johnny Cash really hears her. The darkness of his mind is not gone forever, but the battle with his demonic voices has begun. He has a new voice of hope to conquer the darkness. June has given him a gospel message.

Mary Magdalene witnessed angels. I want to witness angels too. Maybe the first step is to look for them in the midst of our daily lives. An angel is a messenger of life-altering good news. Maybe you, too, have seen one.

13

◌

The Conversation

The longest conversation that Jesus has with a single person takes place in the Gospel of John. It was the middle of the day and Jesus came to a well in Samaria. There he spoke at length with a woman who had been married five times. Jesus revealed to her that he was the Messiah. After his resurrection, Jesus also had in-depth conversations with Peter and with Mary Magdalene. These private conversations between an individual and Jesus are rare and precious.

I think that the most beautiful passage in the Bible is the conversation that Jesus has with Mary Magdalene outside the tomb in the Gospel of John. In the course of this exchange, Jesus not only shows her that he is alive, but he also asks her to preach the gospel.

Seeing

When she had said this, she turned around and saw Jesus standing there, but she did not know that it was Jesus. Jesus said to her, "Woman, why are you weeping? Whom are you looking for?" Supposing him to be the gardener, she said to him, "Sir, if you have carried him away, tell me where you have laid him, and I will take him away."

—JOHN 20:14–15

Mary Magdalene is alone when she sees Jesus, but she doesn't recognize him. She thinks he is the gardener. Scholars have wondered how someone so close to Jesus could have mistaken him for someone else. There are a few possibilities.

It is possible that Jesus was physically changed in the resurrected form. This would make sense as the two disciples on the road to Emmaus in the Gospel of Luke also do not recognize him. Was his appearance altered in some way? Or was it simply the fact that he was bloodied and broken when he died and it was too hard to comprehend his health and vitality? We may never know.

Another possibility is that Mary Magdalene wasn't really looking. She had made up her mind that Jesus was dead. She was looking for a body. She was unable to see him as a living person.

How many times do we fail to see the goodness right in front of us? How many times have we agonized about the difficulties of our life while not seeing the blessings? Suffering can be all-consuming, and it is easy to let the good news slide. Sometimes we must discipline our minds to give thanks, especially when we are in pain. Mary almost lets her pain consume her to the point that she cannot see Jesus. But thank God that Jesus won't allow her to despair. He calls her out of her grief. He calls her to see clearly again. And he does this by calling out her name.

What's In a Name?

> In the beginning was the Word, and the Word was with God, and the Word was God.
>
> —JOHN 1:1

> Jesus said to her, "Mary!"
>
> —JOHN 20:16

There is this incredible scene in the play *The Miracle Worker*. The play is based on the life of Helen Keller and her teacher Annie Sullivan. Helen fell ill as a toddler and completely lost both her sight and her hearing. She lived in a world of darkness and acted like an animal until Annie became her tutor and with dogged determination tried to reach her. Annie was able to force Helen to behave, but she was unable to make Helen understand the connection between the letters she would draw in Helen's palm and the actual meaning of the words, meaning that represented objects and people around her. Helen was unable to connect meaning to the words and, as a result, she was completely alone. She was unreachable.

The miracle happened on a normal day. Annie was following Helen around, giving her rewards for her behavior like one would a dog, but never failing to spell the words into Helen's palm whenever Helen encountered a new object. Helen was at a water pump. As the water fell over her young hands, Annie doggedly spelled out W-A-T-E-R. And something deep inside Helen's mind shifted.

As a toddler, before Helen fell ill, she had learned her first word, wawa, for water. From deep inside the recesses of her mind, Helen remembered this one word and the connection was made between the word that she once knew, the water falling over her hands, and the strange forms that Annie was writing into her palm. In the scene, Helen stops and in her muted, strange voice, tries to speak aloud her first word, "Wawa."

Helen Keller would later write about the nature of this moment: "My darkness has been filled with the light of intelligence."[1]

In that moment, the logos came to Helen. Her mind awakened to the communication that could occur between herself and those around her. She was no longer alone.

It says in the beginning of the Gospel of John that God created the world through the Logos, the Word. It was meaning itself, communication itself that made the creation. It was communication that was the light entering the darkness, the formation of a connection between God and the creation, a movement of love.

The name of God has never really been known to us. To this day, observant Jews do not speak the name of God. They write G-D. When Moses asked for God's name, God told him *I AM WHO I AM.*

We cannot grasp the name of God because a name contains the essence of a thing; it is the logos of the object or person that it represents and God cannot be fully known. So it is no surprise that we cannot truly know God's name. Even Jesus called God

---

1. Helen Keller, "Out of the Dark," the *Cry for Justice: An Anthology of Jovial Protest* (Philadelphia: The John C. Winston Co., 1915), 1.

Abba, which can best be translated as Daddy. And we all know that Daddies do have real names, but their children usually do not call them by their names. Instead, terms of endearment capture their relationship.

We cannot adequately call God by name but God can call us by name. God, in fact, calls us into existence. When we are baptized, our name is used. We are marked as Christ's own, forever using our name. Have you ever really listened when someone that you love called you by your name? The words become so beautiful. You are known.

When Mary Magdalene's eyes were opened to a new reality, it was because God called her by name. The Word was spoken to her, and she heard it. Her mind opened. Like Helen Keller, a connection was made in her understanding. She saw that the one she thought was dead was alive. Everything in her world expanded in that one moment. Her nightmare became full of light. Jesus had risen.

What was the name that Jesus called her? Jesus did not call her "Woman." Jesus did not call her "Friend." Jesus did not even call her by her more formal name "Mary Magdalene." Jesus just said, "Mary." He called her by her simple name. He knew who she was apart from every other woman on the planet. He remembered her. He still remembered her.

Rabbouni

The word that Mary uses to address Jesus gives us enormous insight into their relationship. She calls him Rabbouni, which in Hebrew means "Teacher."

Jesus was her teacher. He was not her husband or her friend or her lover or her partner. He was her teacher. She says it so plainly that it makes me wonder why we have spent so many years supposing alternative kinds of relationships. Is it so hard to imagine that a woman could be a follower of Jesus? Is it so hard to imagine that a woman could be a student of Jesus? Is it so hard to imagine that she loved her teacher, her lord, her master? Is that love any less than sexual love?

Mary does not say, "Oh, my love!" or "My dear husband!" She says, "Rabbouni!" What we call a person tells us a lot about the relationship. Jesus called her Mary. Mary called him Teacher. Jesus taught her about God.

Attachment

> Do not hold on to me, because I have not yet ascended to the Father. . . .
>
> —JOHN 20:17

Some scholars point to these words as evidence that Mary Magdalene did in fact have a sexual relationship with Jesus. Wasn't she about to hold him? I'm afraid that the words are again very vague in the ancient Greek. Was she falling at his feet to hold them? Did she rush to hug him?

In the Gospel of Mark, Mary Magdalene and the other Mary rush towards Jesus when they recognize him and they both fall down and hold onto his feet. Was this what Mary was about to do in John's gospel as well? It was common to fall at the feet of a holy teacher, to hold onto his feet. Perhaps Mary was going to hold Jesus's feet.

What exactly were her physical movements that caused Jesus to stop her? We will never know because John the Evangelist did not think this was worth mentioning.

If we could lay aside our cultural fascination with sex for a moment, we might begin to wonder about something much more profound and mysterious, namely, what exactly was Jesus's physical form when he first appeared to Mary by the tomb? Why could she not touch him? Was his body only partially present?

In many other gospel accounts, the resurrected Jesus eats solid food. He lets Mary Magdalene hold his feet in Mark. He lets Thomas touch his wounds in Luke. So why, in the Gospel of John alone, does Jesus tell Mary not to hold him? Was he in a less solid form? Would she have been able to touch him if she had tried? These questions may never be answered, but they nevertheless are there to remind us of the greatest mystery in the Christian tradition. Jesus returned from the dead, but what exactly was his physical composition? We may never know.

Perhaps Jesus is also telling Mary that she cannot hold onto him on a psychological level as well. It is time for her to continue to be possessed with devotion to Jesus but not to hold onto his physical presence. He releases her from her incessant desire to be near his physical body. He tells her not to hold on any longer.

How hard it is for us to let go of the people we love. We want to stay with them forever, to hold them. This kind of attachment can often mask love. But true love is able to let go.

True love allows the beloved to die if it is their time. True love does not need the other to be physically present at all times. True love grants true freedom. Mary Magdalene was moving on to the highest stage of devotion to God. She no longer needed the physical presence of Jesus with her to know that she was loved. He was asking her to trust that he loved her even when she could not hold him.

The first one to witness the resurrection was also the first one to let him go. She was able to let him go because she realized that he would never really leave her.

14

The First Preacher

Go to my brothers and say to them, "I am ascending to my
Father and your Father, to my God and your God."

—John 20:17

Women were not allowed to testify in court in Jesus's day.
The woman wasn't considered a true person, so her testimony could not be trusted. And demoniacs were social outcasts.
They were not to be seen or heard. This makes Mary Magdalene
the worst possible witness in a court of law.

Jesus chose a woman who had been possessed by demons to
relay the miracle of the resurrection. He chose a single woman
who had most likely battled serious mental health issues as his
first preacher. He chose the least likely person: someone who
was not taken seriously, someone who was shamed, someone
who could not be heard. Why choose a witness that no one
would trust?

The choice of Mary Magdalene as Jesus's first witness is
one of the greatest pieces of evidence that the resurrection came
from God. No rational human being would choose a witness

who was not allowed to testify. From a human perspective, the choice of Mary Magdalene made absolutely no sense.

God did not choose the first witness based on her qualifications or her reputation. She had no qualifications. She had no reputation. No, God chose the person who loved Jesus the most and who never left Jesus's side. Mary Magdalene was the one who God chose because God was, and still is, the one who transforms shame into honor.

There is still so much shame associated with mental illness today. Many people hide their struggles for fear that they will not be taken seriously. It is only very recently, and in certain select circles, that some Americans have admitted to being in therapy. To admit to struggling with any form of mental health issue is to assume a position of great vulnerability in our society today. It is to admit weakness.

I believe that God is speaking to us through the story of Mary Magdalene. God is asking us to learn the truth about her. Couldn't Mary Magdalene be a role model for all those who struggle with mental illness? If God chose Mary Magdalene as the first great witness, then God values all who struggle with mental health issues. And, if we are honest with ourselves, that means all of us.

Her True Name

In the Eastern Orthodox tradition, Mary Magdalene is called by another name, and it is not "prostitute." She is called *Apostola Apostolorum*, "the Apostle to the Apostles."

On June 6, 2016, Pope Francis dedicated a liturgical Feast Day to Saint Mary Magdalene. This kind of Feast Day previously had been given to saints such as Peter and Paul. It is the highest honor for a saint, to be remembered in this way. In his speech, Pope Francis referred to Mary Magdalene as the Apostle to the Apostles. It seems that the time has come for us to reconsider this misunderstood woman and honor her for who she really was.

There is an icon hanging in my office: Mary Magdalene is dressed in red as usual, but this time her clothes are not falling off her body. Instead, she wears a red robe regally, as if she were one of the disciples. She is standing next to Peter, John, and others. Her hand is outstretched as if she is trying to reach the disciples to explain something. Mary Magdalene is relaying the message of the resurrection. She is telling the disciples that Jesus is alive. In this icon, she looks older, wiser, serious, and yet joyful as she relays the message of salvation.

Truly, Mary Magdalene was the apostle to the apostles. An apostle means "one who is sent," and Mary Magdalene was sent by Jesus to tell the others the good news.

Does Mary Magdalene Speak?

There is a strange discrepancy between the gospels. Mark recounts that Mary Magdalene and the other women who witness the resurrection were silent, and that they did not tell the disciples that Jesus had risen because they were afraid. It is true that most women would have been terrified to speak out on such a significant matter. But if the women never spoke, and in Mark there are no other witnesses to the resurrection, then how did the gospel message spread?

In Luke and Matthew, the gospel writers relay that Mary shares the news, but they do not actually recount her words. We don't know exactly what she said to make the disciples listen.

It is only in the Gospel of John that we actually hear Mary Magdalene's voice. Mary Magdalene's final words are:

I have seen the Lord.

—JOHN 20:18

These final words are significant. Her method of sharing the gospel was simply to recount her experience. She makes an "I statement," describing what she had seen. It is simple and straightforward. She models what all Christians are called to do.

How are we supposed to witness? Even the word makes most Christians uncomfortable. Are we supposed to tell people that they are missing something wonderful? Are we supposed to tell them that they need God for salvation? How do we tell people about what Jesus has done for us and yet respect and honor those who listen?

Witnessing simply means telling the truth, telling the story about your relationship with God. Mary does not lecture and she does not judge. She simply relays what she had seen, that Jesus has risen from the dead. She tells people that she has seen him. Her joy overflows. She is simply telling her own story, for her story has become a part of the gospel story. The only way to witness is to tell the story of your relationship with Jesus, just your story and no one else's.

Americans have no inhibitions when it comes to sharing our favorite restaurants, movies, clothing sales, etc. So why do we have so much trouble sharing the news of God's goodness in our lives? Are we afraid to be vulnerable? Ashamed to be faithful? Do we feel that someone will be offended? Why has the simple joy of sharing Jesus gotten lost? How have we forgotten the greatest privilege and the greatest joy of the Christian life?

The First Preacher

When Jesus asked Mary to tell the others that he had risen, Jesus was asking her to preach. When I have questioned my vocation or wondered if God could possibly be calling a woman to be an ordained minister, I have looked to this very passage. Jesus entrusted his message to a woman. He believed in her. And I think that Jesus believes in all of us no matter if we are male or female, rich or poor, black or white. He asks all of us to share how we feel about him. All of us.

15

Mary's Silence

Mary Magdalene never speaks again. After her announcement to the disciples that she has seen the Lord, Mary just seems to disappear. She does not appear at all in the book of Acts. After the four gospels, Mary Magdalene vanishes.

There are gnostic gospels that mention Mary Magdalene. The most famous of these is the Gospel of Mary Magdalene. There is only one copy of this gospel in existence. It was written no earlier than the third century in Egypt. The one document in existence was found in Cairo in 1896. Scholars realized the importance of this text in shedding light on Magdalene. By 2003, Karen L. King published a book called *The Gospel of Mary Magdala: Jesus and the First Woman Apostle*. The Gospel of Mary Magdalene is a fascinating document, but it is not historically reliable. However, it does refer to Mary as an authority, one who teaches Peter, a concept that would not have been welcomed by the later church. Here is a passage from the Gospel of Mary Magdalene:

> Peter said to Mary, "Sister, we know that the Savior loved you more than all other women. Tell us the words of the Savior

that you remember, the things which you know that we don't because we haven't heard them."

Mary responded, "I will teach you about what is hidden from you." And she began to speak these words to them.[1]

After Mary explains her wisdom, Peter complains about the fact that she seems to have been favored by Jesus:

Peter answered and spoke concerning these same things.

He questioned them about the Savior: "Did He really speak privately with a woman and not openly to us? Are we to turn about and all listen to her? Did He prefer her to us?"

Then Mary wept and said to Peter, "My brother Peter, what do you think? Do you think that I have thought this up myself in my heart, or that I am lying about the Savior?"

Levi answered and said to Peter, "Peter you have always been hot tempered.

Now I see you contending against the woman like the adversaries.

But if the Savior made her worthy, who are you indeed to reject her? Surely the Savior knows her very well."[2]

Here Peter struggles with the concept that Mary Magdalene may be chief among the followers of Jesus. Peter, the rock upon which the church is built, finds himself deferring to Mary for wisdom and guidance about Jesus.

---

1. *The Gospel of Mary of Magdala* 5:5–7.

2. *The Gospel of Mary of Magdala* 9:4–8.

The four canonical gospels are believed to have been written within the first century, much closer to the life of Jesus. Ten or fifteen manuscripts were in existence within the first hundred years of the writing of the letters and other documents that would form the New Testament, including some fairly large portions of papyrus, containing significant passages from the gospels or the letters of Paul. By the beginning of the third century, there were at least forty-eight manuscripts in existence. The four gospels are much more reliable because they were written during a time closer to the life of Jesus.[3]

Cynthia Bourgeault, a scholar of Mary Magdalene, has written much about the gnostic texts, but even she admits that there is more than enough material about Mary Magdalene just in the Bible itself. She writes, "Even if we had only these four texts (the four canonical gospels) to work with, there is still more than enough material here to warrant a complete revisioning of Mary Magdalene. The question is not about the information; it's about how we hear and process it. And in the Christian West, sad to say, we have been mostly sleepwalking for nearly two thousand years."[4]

Legends of Magdalene

Legends speak of Mary Magdalene going in two different directions after the resurrection. In one strain of legends, Magdalene

---

3. If you are someone who is intrigued by the gnostic texts, I encourage you to seek out such books as Cynthia Bourgeault's *The Meaning of Mary Magdalene* or the work of Elaine Pagels. Both are excellent authors who dig deep into the gnostic texts.

4. Cynthia Bourgeault, *The Meaning of Mary Magdalene* (Boston: Shambhala, 2010), 5.

goes to Ephesus, and in the other she boards a boat which takes her to France.

In the Eastern Church, the legend has it that Mary Magdalene traveled with Mary the Mother of Jesus to Ephesus and is buried along with Jesus's mother there. This tradition sounds plausible but it begs the question as to why Mary Magdalene is not mentioned as a member of that early church movement whereas Mary Jesus's mother is documented to have been present with the early Christians. Nevertheless, pilgrims who travel to Ephesus will find a tomb there dedicated to Mary Magdalene.

On the Western side of the church, Catholics today believe that Mary Magdalene traveled with Mary of Bethany and Lazarus to France where Magdalene chose to live in a cave for some thirty years. Her body is believed to be buried at the chapel of Saint-Maximin, located in Aix-en-Provence, about 75 miles northeast of Marseille, in the Southeast of France.[5]

There are stories from the Middle Ages of Mary Magdalene entering the woods as a hermit and growing hair all over her body. They called her Hairy Mary. Other stories have her going to France carrying Jesus's baby, as Dan Brown narrates in his book *The Da Vinci Code*. But these are stories, just stories. The Bible's last words about Mary Magdalene are her own words, witnessing to the Risen Christ. From the perspective of the Bible itself, she seems to just disappear.

Like the writers of the gnostic gospels, I too have wondered what happened to Mary Magdalene. Jesus's mother plays a role

---

5. Mike Galli, *Mary Magdalene (1st Century AD)* (London: Kings College History Department, 2005), 1.

in the early church. There are many women who rise to leadership in the earliest days of Christianity. Why would Mary Magdalene not have been among these female leaders in the early church? My only guess is that Mary Magdalene went into a place of deep prayer and devotion after her experience of the Risen Christ. She did what she had been called to do. She spread the gospel to the ones who would then carry it to the ends of the earth. Maybe, after her final words, she just lived in peace.

The gap in our knowledge about Mary Magdalene has led us to create various scenarios as to the remainder of her life. Interestingly, the suppositions about Mary Magdalene have coincided neatly with the church's need to clarify certain topics such as sexual activity and the role of women. Magdalene has been molded to fit the needs of those who lived after her. In an article for *Smithsonian* magazine, James Carroll writes,

> Confusions attached to Mary Magdalene's character were compounded across time as her image was conscripted into one power struggle after another, and twisted accordingly. In conflicts that defined the Christian Church—over attitudes toward the material world, focused on sexuality; the authority of an all-male clergy; the coming of celibacy; the branding of theological diversity as heresy; the sublimations of courtly love; the unleashing of "chivalrous" violence; the marketing of sainthood, whether in the time of Constantine, the Counter-Reformation, the Romantic era, or the Industrial Age—through all of these, reinventions of Mary Magdalene played their role. Her recent reemergence in a novel and film as the secret wife of Jesus and the mother of

his fate-burdened daughter shows that the conscripting and twisting are still going on.[6]

We may never know exactly what happened to this great woman. Perhaps we were left with room to imagine in order for us to fill in the gaps as we needed throughout the centuries. I have always believed that the scriptures do not always tell us all that we want to know, but they do mysteriously tell us exactly what we need to know.

6. *http://www.smithsonianmag.com/history/who-was-mary-magdalene-119565482/#xuSVG9 EfmCVgp6Ib.99.*

16

Learning from Mary

This final chapter is for those who wish to reflect further on the relationship between mental and spiritual health. It can be used for personal reflection or, better still, in small groups. I encourage those who read this chapter to answer the questions at the end of each section in writing and to share their responses with trusted members of a small group or spiritual friends. Let us look to Mary Magdalene as a role model and seek our own mental and spiritual health.

There is still so much shame associated with mental health. Sure, it is hip and cool to say that you are in therapy but no one wants to hear the bad stuff. Depression is boring. Anger issues, well, most people run from that. We all want so badly to tell each other how great we are doing. It is hard to be honest about the fact that our marriage is shaky or that we feel that we no longer know our children.

The church is a good place to begin the work of combatting shame. And we must begin by looking inside our minds, all of us, even those who have never thought about entering the office of a therapist. We must look inside our minds with the understanding that each and every one of us is battling sin in one form or another. The mind is a battlefield and we must be conscious of its landscape if we are to win the war. St. Paul describes the battle in this way,

> For in my inner being I delight in God's law; but I see another law at work in me, waging war against the law of my mind and making me a prisoner of the law of sin at work within me.
>
> —ROMANS 7:22–23

Paul differentiates between the body and the mind. But all thought and impulse originates within the mind. And we cannot ever find our way to the pure love of God without contending with the sin that lives in our minds, or, as Magdalene would have us understand, the temptation and the demons that can find a home within us.

We cannot win this war of the mind without first combatting the shame that keeps our thoughts hidden even from ourselves. We must begin to speak of mental health with honesty, objectivity, and clarity. In short, we must change our mindset about mental health.

Mental health, and spiritual health as the two are so interrelated, is much like physical health. It is a journey, it is an ever-changing complex narrative of the mind, body, and soul. The truth about mental health is that it is not black-and-white. A person is not simply healthy or crazy. Mental health is a story of a human mind and each mind is different, complex, beautiful, and original in every way.

If you are wise, you go to a doctor at least once a year for a physical checkup. The doctor, if he or she is any good at all, does not just pronounce you healthy or sick, the doctor gives you a complex picture of your health. For example, I am in my late 40s. My weight is normal. The doctor suggests that I take calcium, vitamin D, and iron as those vitamins seem low in my bloodstream. Though I exercise regularly, he tells me that it would be best if I started lifting weights because women my age tend to lose bone density quickly and lifting weights can counteract loss of bone density. He talks to me about menopause, as it should come at some point within the next decade. He asks me if I could become pregnant, as that would not be a good idea at my age. What this doctor does is give me a complex narrative about a body that is aging gently and how to care for it. Am I basically healthy right now? Yes. But I have to work on my health, and my physical includes a mammogram so the news might change at any moment. I am healthy, but I am aging and losing bone density and I need some vitamins.

What if we went to a psychotherapist or spiritual director once a year for a similar kind of checkup? If we were to do that, how would we convey the landscape of our mind to the counselor? What are the vital signs? What are the vitamins? What is exercise for the mind? How do we strive to keep ourselves mentally well? Does your mind go through menopause? Does it age? Your mind is organic matter. It is a wonder that we don't look after it better.

What if the church encouraged people to ask one another not just about their physical health but about their mental health as well? This might have to happen in a safe context like a trusted small group or faithful friend, since there is still so much shame and stigma attached that most are not prone to honesty. But what if we truly began to trust each other enough to ask about our mental health as we do about our physical health?

"Have you been worrying much about your brother? Have you been able to turn the worry into prayer? How is your anxiety in the morning? Does meditation help?"

In other words, maybe the goal of Christian community should be to love one another more honestly and thoroughly by trusting each other with our mental health struggles and needs. If we can bring Mary Magdalene out of shame and hiding, then perhaps we could help other people to become aware of their minds and to begin to care for their own mental and spiritual health.

How does one learn to articulate one's mental health? So much of the work of our minds is left undiagnosed, hidden even from ourselves. Let's begin by figuring out how you and I could keep better track of our thoughts and feelings. What are the vital signs of feelings? How can we begin to describe the landscape of our minds?

Scripture tells us that the mind is the place where temptation begins and that this temptation can become obsession or addiction or a demon as the New Testament language would describe it. The mind is also the place where God speaks, inspiration occurs, and new ideas are born. So how can we clear the way through the obsessive, repetitive thoughts and carve out a blank canvass for God to speak to us? How can we clean up our minds so that there is some room for God?

It takes strength and courage to listen to the landscape of your mind. It is a lot like exercise. It takes commitment and the ability to be honest with oneself. Where do your thoughts roam? What do you think about when you wake up in the morning? How do your moods progress? Do you need help managing your moods? To actually look at these mental health signposts is difficult for many. How do we begin?

Look for Joy

Joy is very different from happiness. Joy does not involve one particular mood but rather it is a state in which a person is able to relish in the goodness of God's creation. One can be joyful in almost any circumstance, even when one is grieving. Joy is a state in which one basks in the presence of God. Ask yourself this simple question, "Do I find joy in life?" If so, when and where do you find that joy? Is there a way to increase your access to whatever it is that brings you joy? Joy is a sign of the presence of God. How can you bring yourself into that presence with more frequency?

John writes of finding joy in the presence of friends and fellow believers:

> I have much to write to you, but I do not want to use paper and ink. Instead, I hope to visit you and talk with you face to face, so that our joy may be complete.
>
> —2 JOHN 1:13 NIV

John clearly found joy in being with people who loved Jesus. He could share with them what had been happening in his life, his journeys to spread the gospel, and that would make him joyful.

What is your inner nature? Do you find joy from being in the presence of people you love? Do you find joy from being alone in the presence of God? Are you, like me, one who fits in between introversion and extraversion and needs a balance of both time with God alone and time with friends? The company that you keep affects your mental health tremendously. It is essential that you find a community of faith and foster relationships of trust within that community if you are to find and sustain joy. Once you have the anchor of joyful and loving relationships, then you can venture out into the broken world and minister to those in pain, those who are despairing or angry or even suicidal. But you must anchor yourself to joy in God and others before venturing into the darkness to do God's work. Remember that Jesus tended to send his disciples out two by two so that they could take joy in each other.

Perhaps you are a person who finds joy in your work. Perhaps you are an artist, a sculptor, a painter. Maybe you take joy in music, dance or theater, sports or games. One does not have to be particularly adept at any of these things to enjoy them. Do you realize that having fun, taking joy in life, is good for your mental and physical health? So long as you are not abusing others to get there or hurting your body or taking unnecessary risks, it is good to take joy in life. Remember that Jesus's first miracle was at a party. (Weddings then were major parties that tended to last about a week!)

Perhaps you take joy in nature. You see the beauty of God's creation and it sustains you. If that is the case, make sure that you search and find that place on this planet where you can access that joy and beauty. It is not just a hobby. It is you taking care of your mental and spiritual health.

We must pursue joy. Find it. Nurture it. Identify it and, perhaps most of all, give thanks for it. Joy is a gift from God and it is nourishment for the soul and mind.

Never underestimate the power and presence of joy. It can change lives. It is desirable and can make a person well. In the book of Hebrews, it says that Jesus even went to the cross for the sake of joy:

> . . . fixing our eyes on Jesus, the pioneer and perfecter of faith. For the joy set before him he endured the cross, scorning its shame, and sat down at the right hand of the throne of God.
>
> —HEBREWS 12:2 NIV

This indicates that the joy Jesus experienced was so great as to not only trump the cross but make the cross something that could be scorned, laughed at. Who would not want to tap into such joy? But unfortunately, the majority of people cannot experience joy because their mind is full of obstacles to joy. Let us look more closely at those obstacles so that we can learn to cast them aside and make more room for joy.

Questions to Ponder:

1. What brings you joy in life? Where is your greatest satisfaction?

2. How can you increase your exposure to those things that bring you joy?

3. How can you literally fight for and protect the joy in your life? How have you failed to do this at times and how can you resolve to do better?

Exploration of Memory

Most of the great obstacles, demons, or destructive thoughts that cloud the human mind take root in childhood. If one is to venture into the journey of mental health, one has no other choice but to revisit the memories of childhood: the good, the bad, and the ugly. Children are in an open spiritual state. Trauma and neglect, guilt and fear—all can imprint the child's brain in deep and profound ways. The child will learn to adapt and cope with the dysfunction and destruction that surround it, but the coping mechanism itself can be the element that brings about later mental health issues. The coping mechanism can become a perceived reality, a pattern that the adult lives into, a pattern that no longer serves in an adult world, a pattern that can serve as an obstacle to joy.

Judy was a pudgy girl. She knew that her mother was embarrassed by her weight. Even as a little girl, her mother would make comments about her big belly, her heavy legs. She would comment on how pretty and petite other girls looked. She would crack jokes about her fatty, her little "pudgeball." She would look at her daughter with eyes of criticism. By the time that Judy was about eleven, she realized that she could refuse her appetite. She began to diet and, predictably, her body grew thinner. She was met with much praise and even surprise from her mother. At first the dieting was welcome. It impressed her mother that she had discipline, that she could say no to food. But the dieting worsened. Slowly, Judy became an anorexic. She enjoyed the feeling of control that it gave her to refuse food. And she enjoyed being thinner than her mother. Most of all, she enjoyed the worry and even alarm that it created in her mother. Judy was angry, very angry, and starving herself seemed to be the best way to express the rage inside her. And so a childhood memory, of feeling fat and being told she was fat, was twisted into an alternative reality, in which a girl who was healthy and beautiful began to abuse her body. Judy would end up hospitalized before she began the painful work of addressing her anorexia; her mother would learn the hurt she had instilled in her daughter so early on. Together, they had to face the memories that Judy had of her mother's constant criticism. They had to bring the memories into the light, study them and then heal them.

In Judy's case, her mother had suffered similar criticisms from her own mother. When treatment began, Judy's mother was strong enough and willing enough to look at herself. She told Judy how sorry she was, that she loved Judy's body just as God had made it. Her criticisms of her daughter were really more like echoes of how her mother spoke to her, criticizing her appearance constantly and making her feel inadequate. Because Judy's mother had not dealt with these memories of her own mother's criticism, she handed the pain on blindly to her daughter. Generations can pass on sin and pain to generations if no one does the work of seeking out and healing those memories. Even the ancients knew of generational sin. Moses explained that God spreads sin across generations by "visiting the iniquity of the parents upon the children and the children's children, to the third and the fourth generation" (Exodus 34:7).

One can heal memories in the same way that Mary Magdalene was healed of her demons, by bringing them into the presence of Jesus and asking for healing. Take Jesus with you into the most painful parts of your childhood or adolescence. Bring him with you and let him hold you. Ask him to command the demons to leave. Absorb his love for you even in the midst of the brokenness. This is a kind of meditative exercise that can be done over and over again, each time a painful memory is unearthed. And the healing of your own mind and heart will bless your children's children.

Questions to Ponder:

1. What are the memories from your childhood that still cause you pain? Even the most loving of families encounters struggle or difficulty. When did you first feel injustice or hurt? How did you respond as a child and how has your learned response become part of how you act today?

2. Have you ever tried to speak to your loved ones about painful memories, not with blame or shame in mind, but as a way to bring the suffering into the light, as a path to forgiveness? Is this something that could still be done?

2. Meditate on these most painful memories and bring Jesus with you. Ask him to cast out the darkness. Ask him to hold you in the midst of the pain. Experience the miraculous healing power of his love as many times as you need to. This mediation may be practiced over and over again.

Observing Your Thoughts

As he thinks in his heart, so is he.

—PROVERBS 23:7 NKJV

Do not be conformed to this world, but be transformed by the renewing of your minds, so that you may discern what is the will of God—what is good and acceptable and perfect.

—ROMANS 12:2

Dr. Caroline Leaf is an Australian neuroscientist. She is doing remarkable work on how to observe and change your thought patterns. Her theory is that the mind is separate from the brain. The mind, being the intention and will of a person, can override the pattern of the brain. In other words, as St. Paul once wrote, it really is possible to renew your mind. We can train our minds to focus on the will of God, on the doing of justice and the pursuit of truth. We can clear our minds of toxic thinking and destructive mindsets that lead to bad behavior. The will of a person, with the help of God, can do these things. Our minds are flexible and adaptable and they will respond to the will of the person who hosts them.

Dr. Leaf writes, "You are free to make choices about how you focus your attention, and this affects how the chemicals and proteins and wiring of your brain change and function. Scientists are proving that the relationship between what you think and how you understand yourself—your beliefs, dreams, hopes, and thoughts—has a huge impact on how your brain works."[1]

1. Caroline Leaf, *Switch on Your Brain: The Key to Peak Happiness, Thinking and Health* (Grand Rapids, MI: Baker Books, 2013), 33.

In other words, the thoughts that you entertain affect and influence the architecture of your brain. Negative thoughts can breed more negative thoughts and eventual thought patterns. Love and joy can breed more love and joy. It is the will that turns the brain from the destructive thought patterns to those that are healing. Mind over matter really is true, the will can affect and influence the physical matter of the brain.

But before we can influence our thoughts, we must learn to listen to them accurately and honestly. The best way that I know to listen clearly and accurately to your thoughts is to either write them down verbatim or to speak them aloud.

When I was in my early twenties, I spent a year in psychoanalysis. My father's debilitating depression during my childhood had produced a kind of anxiety and worry in me that was almost paralyzing. I realized that if I were to become a functioning adult, I was going to have to figure out how to manage my worries. My parents were very supportive and helped me pay for the treatment. For about nine months, I lay on a sofa four times a week for an hour and I talked and talked.

Psychoanalytic treatment involves the simple practice of speaking your thoughts aloud. As you lay on the sofa, the analyst is not to be visible to you so that you are not distracted or influenced by their facial expressions or reactions. The analyst sits behind you or to the side. And you just look up at the ceiling and you let your thoughts become verbalized.

Over the months, I heard myself think. It was an incredible gift that changed my life. I am so thankful for the gentle, kind woman who saw me and listened to these thoughts with me week after week. Perhaps the most important thing I realized was that I was a good person. I had not known that before. I heard how much I loved others. I analyzed my worries and I marveled at how incredibly repetitive they were. I learned that certain thoughts were signs that I was frightened. I learned how to combat that fear.

Ideally, psychoanalysis takes about four years. I did not have the resources for such an endeavor, but just one year provided me with the key that I needed to begin to hear my thoughts. Even to this day, if I am troubled about something or upset, I will take some time alone to talk aloud to God, listening to the patterns of my thoughts, or I will write my thoughts down. Like broken records, destructive thoughts or anxiety are unoriginal and can easily occupy our minds if we let them. But once we identify them, these thoughts can become background noise or even subtle distractions. They never go away permanently, but they no longer have the strength to occupy so much space in our minds.

For me, morning prayer and exercise are vital. My most fearful and destructive worries will most often waken with me in the morning. The words of scripture are like balm to a frightened soul. The ancient prayers that my tradition speaks daily are like living waters cooling the heat of my mind. Scripture and prayer anchor me to health, they draw the mind away from its restless wanderings and back into the solid arms of God. Scripture is my salve, my beauty. It beckons my mind to the light.

Exercise is also helpful when it comes to quieting the mind. Jogging and yoga are my favorites. Since my days involve lots and lots of people, I prefer to exercise quietly, to give my mind time to roam and rejuvenate. While the body is physically challenged, the mind has time to process. Exercise is a much-neglected tool for mental health.

Here is some documentation from the National Institute of Health:

> An essential component of lifestyle modification is exercise. The importance of exercise is not adequately understood or appreciated by patients and mental health professionals alike. Evidence has suggested that exercise may be an often-neglected intervention in mental health care. Aerobic exercises, including jogging, swimming, cycling, walking, gardening, and dancing, have been proved to reduce anxiety and depression.[2]

Not only is exercise beneficial for your brain, but it gives the mind a chance to observe the thoughts while the body is otherwise occupied. For many Americans, sitting still in silent meditation is just too difficult. Our brains have become so stimulated, our thoughts so fast-paced, that it is nearly impossible to make sense of the jumble of thoughts that pour down upon the person who is unaccustomed to sitting still. It is much easier to occupy a portion of the brain with exercise and then use the opportunity to observe the thoughts that traverse the brain during that time. Repetitive thoughts will make themselves known. Distractions will be lessened as the brain has something to occupy its attention. You can hear your thoughts more clearly when you exercise.

---

2. Ashish Sharma, Vishal Madaan, and Frederick D. Petty, "Exercise for Mental Health," *The Primary Care Companion to the Journal of Clinical Psychiatry* 8 (2006): 106.

Listening to the thoughts is considered an advanced form of prayer. It takes courage to bring your thoughts into the light, into the presence of God. The process of observing thought patterns takes great honesty and patience. One has to be able to understand and still love oneself even when the most onerous, selfish, petty, and even malicious thoughts occupy our minds. But we cannot learn the nature of our own demons if we pretend that they do not exist. We have only to look to Mary Magdalene to see that there is hope for all of us who are consumed by destructive thoughts and behaviors.

Forgiveness

> For if you forgive others their trespasses, your heavenly father will also forgive you.
>
> —MATTHEW 6:14

Forgiveness is an essential component of mental and spiritual health. One cannot find the peace of God while harboring resentment or seeking revenge. But forgiveness is quite often misunderstood. Many believe that to forgive means to forget or to have good feelings about someone. Both are false and even damaging concepts. Forgiveness has nothing to do with feelings and it has nothing to do with oblivion or forgetting.

Forgiveness is a process of handing pain and injustice over to God. Human nature would have us hold onto a process that hurts us. Memories, especially trauma, stick to the brain like glue and can alter its functioning. Forgiveness involves no longer holding on to the person who has wronged you, but setting your mind free to live and move again. Forgiveness is the opposite of bondage, it is the liberation of a person. Resentment, obsessive anger, plaguing self-pity—these can be right responses to terrible situations but they can cripple a person, leaving no room for the Spirit of God to move. Forgiveness involves breaking the chains of the mind so that we can listen to God once more, creating space in the landscape of your thoughts for the Holy Spirit to be revealed in you.

Forgiveness, like so many other aspects of the spiritual life, is an original process. In others words, what helps one person forgive might not help you at all. It is up to you to discover how to forgive. Some must confront the one who has wronged them. Others find writing a letter helps, even if it is not ever sent. Still others find that spending time in nature helps or seeking the advice of a counselor or even praying for that person who has hurt you. You must explore how your mind best learns to forgive and follow the process that best suits your needs. Each individual must carve his or her own path to forgiveness.

The length of the process of forgiveness is also completely subjective. Some people are able to forgive quickly. For others it takes concerted effort and much time. If the person or persons who have hurt you are observably sorry, that can help immensely. If that person shows no remorse, the process of forgiveness can be more difficult and can take much longer. Time is a friend to forgiveness as it tends to dull pain. Over time, one is often able to forgive more than one thought possible.

Perhaps the hardest kind of forgiveness is forgiveness of the self. Many people are holding themselves captive without realizing it, nurturing old mistakes and secretly hating themselves for the mistakes they have made. All of us are sinners and all of us have made serious mistakes. Listen to Paul when he writes,

> For I do not understand my own actions. For I do not do what I want, but I do the very thing I hate.
>
> —ROMANS 7:15

If Paul himself felt this way even after his conversion, then we are in good company. All human beings are limited and we find ourselves unable to act as we wish. We have bad moods, unexplained quirks, and poor decision-making abilities. It is inevitable that all people who are introspective at all will find the need to forgive themselves. This is where the grace of God and the love of God are essential to us. It is a great mystery why God chose to send Jesus to save us, but the fact is that God does in fact love us. And no matter how many mistakes we make, that love is still accessible. Grace awaits even the worst criminal. In a sense, our mistakes are simply not large enough, not powerful enough to impact God's love for us. Not even the crucifixion of Jesus could stop God from loving us. We have been forgiven and there is nothing we can do but accept that forgiveness and, in turn, learn to forgive others.

Questions to Ponder:

1. What do you need forgiveness for? How can you begin the process of seeking forgiveness?

2. What weighs on your heart and mind? Is there someone who has wronged you? How can you liberate yourself and

find it in your heart to forgive? Be specific about the plans that you will make to begin that vital process.

3. How can you best experience the ultimate forgiveness and grace of God? What makes this grace known to you?

Prayer

If there is anything that Mary Magdalene can teach us, it is the simple lesson that proximity to Jesus results in greater mental and spiritual health. Taking time to pray, in whatever way seems most life-giving to you, will have great results. Meditating on scripture, walking or running while saying prayers, sitting in silence, even cleaning or writing while praying—all of these things draw the mind and heart to God. And it is God alone who is the ultimate healer of all pain, sadness, and grief. All that we need to do is come into God's presence with an open heart and mind and God will begin the healing process.

I encourage you to seek wellness of the mind as you seek health in your physical body. Look to prayer as a source of strength. As exercise or good nutrition can fuel the body's health and build its strength, so prayer and meditation can strengthen the mind and soul. And remember that just as the body can be wounded, so the mind and heart can suffer wounds as well. If you have lost a job, or someone you love has died, if you have been in a painful conflict with a loved one or you find yourself lonely, be gentle with your mental and spiritual health. The mind will recover just as the body recovers but we do not ask a runner to jog on a sprained ankle and I would not demand spiritual rigor from yourself if you have recently been hurt. Wounds take time to heal, both in body and in mind.

Finally, look to one another. Build relationships of trust and love. God will speak to you through the wisdom of others. One cannot see one's body clearly and neither can we see clearly the working of our own minds. Trust in others. Do not be afraid to get feedback and advice from those you trust. Rely on the strength and perspective of the people who love God with you, just as Mary did.

I trust that together we will journey with Magdalene on a road that leads to resurrection life and hope.

Being Healed

I will never forget the look of that young woman, Kathy, who sat in my office tormented by demons of self-hatred and depression. I wish that I could have shared Mary Magdalene's life with her. I wish that I could have told her how God took a woman who was in bondage and turned her into the first preacher. And if God could do this with Mary Magdalene, God can do it with all of us. There is no one that God cannot reach, no one who is without hope.

We all struggle with mental health. Like physical health, mental health is something that we strive for, something that takes work and growth. There is no standing still. We must strive to be well every moment of every day. We battle temptation constantly. In a troubled world, a world of worry, of violence and of pain, to be human is to grapple with temptation, with fear, and with dark thoughts. To be human is to work constantly at the mysterious balance which is health.

Is it possible to draw a definitive line between mental, physical, and spiritual health? Where does one discipline end and the other begin? Jesus healed people in every way. He healed them in body, in mind, and in spirit. Mary Magdalene was healed as a whole person.

Mary Magdalene suffered, this we know. Exactly how her demons manifested, we may never know. But we do know that she was healed, and her subsequent behavior as a provider for Jesus, her faithfulness and her vulnerability, led her to witness the greatest miracle of all time. Mary Magdalene shows us how to allow ourselves to be healed by God.

How do we know when we are healed? I suppose when, like Mary Magdalene, our lives become dedicated to the service of God. Ironically, we become most healthy when we put God above ourselves, when our health no longer is our first priority.

Mary Magdalene shows us that God does not value us less because we struggle. For God, there is no shame for the mentally ill. In fact, it is our struggles that form us into the people that God calls us to be. Our wounds make us who we are.